dog breeding

Formerly **dog breeders' handbook** now EXPANDED with 48 pages of color photos

Products of man's ability to control genetic material and, by selection, mold breed type toward a specific utilitarian purpose. The Afghan and the Saluki are sight or gaze hounds, bred from earliest times to run down game for the huntsman through their incredible speed of foot.

dog breeding

Formerly **dog breeders' handbook**
now expanded with 48 pages of
color photos

by

ERNEST H. HART

•

*illustrations and cover
designed by the author*

•

Distributed in the U.S.A. by T.F.H. Publications, Inc., 211 West Sylvania Avenue, P.O. Box 27, Neptune City, N.J. 07753; in England by T.F.H. (Gt. Britain) Ltd., 13 Nutley Lane, Reigate, Surrey; in Canada to the book store and library trade by Clarke, Irwin & Company, Clarwin House, 791 St. Clair Avenue West, Toronto 10, Ontario; in Canada to the pet trade by Rolf C. Hagen Ltd., 3225 Sartelon Street, Montreal 382, Quebec; in Southeast Asia by Y.W. Ong, 9 Lorong 36 Geylang, Singapore 14; in Australia and the south Pacific by Pet Imports Pty. Ltd., P.O. Box 149, Brookvale 2100, N.S.W., Australia. Published by T.F.H. Publications, Inc. Ltd., The British Crown Colony of Hong Kong.

". . . and on elfin wings
she brings the promise of spring."

CONTENTS

Foreword 8

CHAPTER 1

EVOLUTION AND SELECTION... 11

How the canine race formed . . . The first true dogs . . . Man
shapes the dog's destiny . . . Darwin's "Origin of Species," explains
evolution . . . Man's search to find the key to inheritance.

CHAPTER 2

THE RIDDLE OF INHERITANCE SOLVED............................. 27

Mendel's discovery of the laws of inheritance . . . Mendel's
"Units" . . . Dominants and recessives . . . Mendelian expectation
chart . . . Mendel's formula . . . His papers lost . . . Theories of
other prominent scientists . . . Mendel's papers found and
his theory given to the world.

CHAPTER 3

GENES, CHROMOSOMES AND CELLS..................................... 37

False genetic theories . . . Mendel's unseen "units" found . . .
Fruit fly experiments . . . Location of genes on chromosomes . . .
Gene linkage . . . The sex chromosomes . . . What genes are
. . . What chromosomes are . . . What cells are . . . How cells
divide . . . Sex-linked characters . . . Chemistry of genes . . .
Mutations . . . Crossing-over . . . Epistasy . . . Partial dominance
. . . Hostile environment . . . DNA and RNA.

CHAPTER 4

GENETICS AND THE DOG BREEDER..................................... 73

The genotype . . . The phenotype . . . Limits of canine inheritable
material . . . Homozygous breed traits . . . Dominant and recessive
traits . . . Simplifying complicated genetics for the breeder's
use . . . Rules governing dominant and recessive traits . . . How
to improve . . . Small genetic advances . . . Correlating factors.

CHAPTER 5

BASIC BREEDING TECHNIQUES... 105

Upgrading . . . Essential breeding traits . . . Variation of germ
plasm . . . Inbreeding . . . Phases of Inbreeding . . . Parallel results
. . . What inbreeding does . . . Results . . . Backcrossing . . . Line-
breeding . . . Varied intensity . . . Results . . . Outcross breeding . . .
Compensation . . . Results . . . Back-massing . . . Heterosis . . .
Hypothesis.

CHAPTER 6

THE BROOD BITCH... 137

Structure . . . Quality . . . Female organs . . . The breeding cycle
. . . First signs . . . The time to breed . . . Ovulation . . . Vaginal
smear . . . How to breed . . . Gestation period . . . Two sires, one
litter . . . Feeding during gestation . . . Determining pregnancy . . .
Whelping preparations . . . Hormones . . . Labor . . . Whelping
. . . Ills during gestation and after whelping.

CHAPTER 7

THE STUD DOG... 155

Importance of stud . . . Fertility . . . How often to use . . . Selection
of stud . . . Care of stud . . . Male organs . . . Orchidism . . .
Fertility drugs.

CHAPTER 8

SELECTION OF BREEDING PARTNERS... 165

The bitch . . . Rating charts . . . Selection of the stud . . . Developing
a strain . . . Rules . . . Compensatory strain.

CHAPTER 9

THE MECHANICS OF BREEDING... 173

Copulation . . . The bitch's role . . . The stud's role . . . The
sperm . . . The eggs . . . How fertilization occurs . . . Aiding the
animals . . . The "tie" . . . Fertilization without sexual fusion . . .
Movement of the ova . . . Artificial insemination . . . Sterility
. . . Vitamins essential to reproduction.

CHAPTER 10

THE RESULTS OF BREEDING 181

Phantom pregnancy . . . Resorption of fetuses . . . Cells and puppies . . . Bitches diet . . . Opening of whelps' eyes—deductions . . . Multiple matings . . . Progeny born . . . Dewclaws . . . Bleeding . . . Selection.

CHAPTER 11

ENVIRONMENT AND HEREDITY 189

Environment selects . . . Environment and heredity working together . . . Forming of species . . . Balance in nature . . . Survival . . . How genetic change can fit new environment . . . The modern breeder . . . Selection for a wanted change . . . Recessives and mutations bring change . . . Natural selection versus man-made selection . . . How to bring change into your strain.

CHAPTER 12

THE IMPORTANCE OF PEDIGREE 201

What a pedigree is . . . What it isn't . . . What a pedigree lacks . . . How to expand our knowledge of the pedigree . . . Typical and atypical . . . Falsifications . . . Card-index system . . . Photos . . . A pedigree of meaning . . . The future.

GLOSSARY OF GENETIC TERMS 210

BIBLIOGRAPHY 212

INDEX 213

FOREWORD

When I was asked by my publisher to write this book on dog breeding I was immediately faced with a physical rather than a mental or occupational problem. How much of all that is now known of the many phases of the subject should I include? How small or how large in scope should this book be? After pondering the subject for no little time I subsequently decided that it must encompass all that is known or associated with the breeding of dogs that it would be possible for me to find, through research into scientific lore on the subject and through poring over my own catalogued and completely objective data, anent canine reproduction, amassed over the years. In other words this book, I resolved, had to be complete in all the many phases of its subject matter.

The amount of information I finally faced was rather staggering in size and scope; and it had all to be judiciously selected from, reworked and translated, and molded into some semblance of narrative form to lend it interest beyond the latitude of its bare material. Only through compressing theories, thoughts and proven practices into the fewest possible meaningful words without corrupting or subtracting from their purpose, have I been able to keep this handbook on breeding under physical control.

Other books have been written encompassing the same premise; good, bad, and indifferent books that can be variously catalogued though within the sphere of the same subject. There are scientific treatises and mountains of scientific papers on various phases of reproduction that are so recondite that they are beyond the understanding of the ordinary breeder, or at least so profound as to be exasperatingly difficult to grasp for anyone not engaged in parallel work or research. Within this complex of reality which is scientifically perceptible and caters completely to objective reality, the area of layman perception becomes greatly and progressively diminished. Such reports are definitely not for the individual interested in breeding and breed improvement as a relaxing sport or hobby.

There are other books on dog breeding so non-objective in approach that they emerge as merely opinionated argument, the written expressions of an individual's ego, a person whose experience, generally with one breed, has led him along unlighted paths of breeding endeavor that end in a black cave of confused conceit. All too frequently arguments can be rationalized to fit what seems to the layman a reasonable pattern of procedure. Such writers construct psuedo-intellectual hypotheses to enable their system of reference to accommodate their half truths and ask us to accept their contradictions.

Since books about dogs and dog breeding are generally written by people who are not vocationally writers, there is a lack of clarity in presentation, disorganization and, other than in scientific treatises, a definite lack of basic subject research, but a fund of nonobjective opinion. As a professional in the field of publication I feel that I can avoid such errors and gather the necessary information into an orderly, pithily presented, interesting and useful book. What you read here, therefore, is never opinion or supposition. These are facts, for I feel that this book would have no value if either of us expected less than the truth. We, I the writer and you the reader, must meet on a common ground of trust and understandable reality or the purpose of this book is lost.

Like the critic viewing a superb piece of abstract art from the hand of a master, the modern breeder must look and absorb external form and, penetrating it, light with the lamp of knowledge the genetic processes that are the base and cause of it. In this way, and only in this way, can he advance and reach toward greater breeding sureness and success in the future.

Ernest H. Hart
Oakdale,
Massachusetts

Breeding better dogs is both a science and an art.
The end result of breeding knowledge is, like this
family of Belgian Tervuren, the kind of sculptured
beauty and conformational perfection that brings
pride to the heart of the breeder.

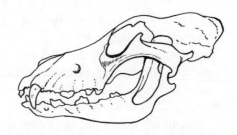

CHAPTER 1

EVOLUTION AND SELECTION

Breeding dogs, or any other mammal, toward a given ideal or standard of perfection, for utilitarian purpose or mere beauty is accomplished, in essence, by controlling the evolution of the specific breed selected and fashioning it, by genetic manipulation and environmental control, into a predestined pattern.

To explain how this can be done, the tools that are available to you, a layman, and the way they and all other information pertinent to the subject of breeding better dogs can be used to your best advantage, is the purpose of this book.

But before we utilize any of this knowledge we must first know more about the species canine, of which our breed is a part, so that we can more fully appreciate the processes of evolution, selection, and environment, that are the natural tools which nature has handed down to us, the new custodians of the canine race.

In a time too long ago for the human mind to fully understand, approximately forty million years ago, the species canine had begun to develop on a plastic, forming earth. The giants of scale and sinew, reptilian monsters of fantastic and fearful mein, had been too limited in genetic scope and had failed to mutate to meet changing environmental demands. So those horrendous kings of the Earth were swept away by the several phases of the ice age. But, during the almost unending Mesozoic era that echoed to the roars of these giants as they ate themselves into oblivion, dramatic mutations were occurring within the germ plasm of smaller, lesser creatures, as nature clumsily experimented in a frantic attempt to perpetuate life on the planet Earth.

Skeletal changes took place, body scales changed to fur and feathers, some reptiles displayed greater energy than their slow moving and almost brainless kin, and certain others began to develop warm blood. The seat of greater reaction to stimuli shifted from the spinal ganglia to the brain and the proportions of this living mass of transitional forms began to change. These resulting strange creatures were the precursors of the various coming animal families of Earth, including the mammalian, viviparous, hair-bearing, milk-giving, intelligent animals that were destined to become the dominant life forms of this whole world.

During the Paleocene age mammalian carnivores began to reach definition as animal entities. Living furtively in the primeaval forests amid the teeming, awesome animal population of a humanless Earth during the twenty million years of the Eocene period that followed, the mammals began to segregate and specialize. Those millions of years of stretched and painful genesis finally fashioned, along with rodents and cat-creatures, the dog-like Mesonyx.

The Oligocene period of the Cenozoic era saw the more primitive mammals become the victims of their own organic simplicity and, due to their inability to cope with a changing world, they became extinct. Meanwhile in the evolving gene-pool of the primitive flesh eaters small, beneficial mutations occurred that gave rise to varied sub-speces within the wide carnivorous evolutionary format. Some of these forms were more capable of adapting to environmental change with greater facility than others and it was from these more plastic species that two great modern groups of meat-eaters began to emerge into the light of easy recognition; the solitary stalking cats and the

Miacis, a small, tree-dwelling, carnivorous mammal, from whom flowed a veritable tide of mammalian genetic material that diversified through the long ages to eventually crystalize into many carnivorous families including that of the dog and wolf.

Tomarctus, long, low, and savage, was the first true canine, the prototype dog that was the direct ancestor of the family **Canidae** that included wolves, coyotes, jackals, foxes, and associated mammals.

dogs, the latter specializing in pack pursuit of their quarry.

The ancestor of the canine family of which we previously wrote, Miacis, who lived approximately forty million years ago, long before the curious simian creature that was the ancestor of mankind crept from the sheltering tree limbs to the floor of social consciousness, was a tree climbing mammal. A strange looking creature who was "neither fish nor fowl", or rather, neither dog nor bear, though ancestor to both, Miacis was small, furtive, arboreal, and probably nocturnal.

Thirty million years later, as the varied hosts of animal life moved sluggishly along their diverse evolutionary paths into the final clear specie focus we know today, a descendent of Miacis, Cynodictis, the grandfather of the canine family, stalked his small prey through the lush underbrush of a primitive world. Still not truly a dog, from Cynodictis there branched many mammalian families that eventually, in the crucible of the ages, took concrete form as bears, cats, raccoons, wolves, hyenas and seals. Finally, a product of random selection from this varied mammalian stock represented by the ubiquitous Cynodictis, there emerged the father of the family canine, the prototype dog, Tomarctus, a predacious, short-legged, true canine who roamed the Earth about fifteen million years ago. Tomarctus was, in turn, the ancestor of wolves, coyotes, jackals, foxes and like canine creatures, as well as of the dog. Permit me here to explain that the time element mentioned throughout is roughly correct but not actually pin-pointed since, though I have been in the dog "game" for a goodly spell, these events took place before my time.

In direct descent from Tomarctus (during the Miocene era) and representing the most important cleavage in canine geneology, there appeared the four protoype breeds of canines, Canis Familiaris, Metris-Optimae, Canis Familiaris Intermedius, Canis Familiaris Leineri, and Canis Familiaris Inostranzewi. These four basic canines were the fountainheads from which flowed, in rough form, all the types of dogs we know today. From the first came the sheep-herding breeds beginning with the early Persian herd dogs; the second proto-type canine produced dogs which eventually emerged as hauling, hunting and toy breeds (the Toy breeds descending from the early Egyptian "House dog"); the third was the basis from which came our sight hounds, again through an ancient Egyptian breed of Greyhound; and from Inostranzewi, the last of the imperishable quartette, came both the powerful Mastiff-type canines and many of our water-dog breeds.

These categories are necessarily broad in concept, because so many of the popular canine breeds of today are the result of an intermingling of the genetic qualities of breeds that descended from the four basic types named above. But all breeds, from the tiny Chihuahua to the massive St. Bernard, from the English Bulldog to the Irish Wolf-

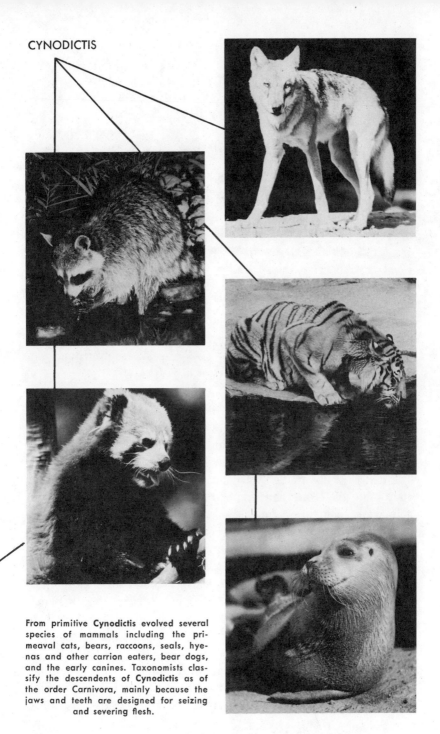

CYNODICTIS

From primitive **Cynodictis** evolved several species of mammals including the primeaval cats, bears, raccoons, seals, hyenas and other carrion eaters, bear dogs, and the early canines. Taxonomists classify the descendents of **Cynodictis** as of the order Carnivora, mainly because the jaws and teeth are designed for seizing and severing flesh.

An early type of small Egyptian house dog and pet. A long and ancient genetic cord stretches from this extinct breed to many of our modern dogs.

hound, are one species. That they can be interbred certifies to this fact. The bewildering diversity of sizes, shapes, conformation and inherent abilities are evidence of the touch of man.

Nature, through millions of years of evolution, produced Tomarctus, the progenitor, and the four basic dog types that spawned slight variety in the canine species. Man then molded the species canine to his own wants, controlling the evolutionary process of the dog through selection.

Initially the dog probably acted as a scavenger, carrying away and consuming the bones and bits of rancid meat that insensitive and animalistic man threw outside his cave entrance. Removal of this garbage and refuse relieved his crude dwelling place of some of the stench that had always pervaded it, and perhaps kept his enemies, both two and four footed, from sniffing him out. It is possible that man came even to appreciate the state of comparative cleanliness achieved through the wild dog's ability to scavenge. If so it is not beyond the realm of imagination to assume that the dog, in that long ago time, subtly helped in the evolution of man, from beast-man, to man-beast.

Eventually the dog followed man on the hunt, then led the hunt when man recognized the value of the animal's greater scenting and hearing ability. It was but a step then for the sluggishly developing

The classical canine comparison of size to indicate extremes in modern breeds. The St. Bernard, the heaviest of breeds (though not the tallest), weighs approximately 185 pounds, while the two Chihuahuas together weigh less than six pounds.

brain of man to perceive and understand that some dogs were better hunters than others and to subsequently select hunting dogs in the image of those that were the best at this very necessary occupation. Man then took another step forward, a giant step. He conceived the idea of breeding the best hunting dog stud to the best hunting dog bitch to produce fine animals for the chase and, when he did, he became the first breeder of dogs for a purpose and took upon himself the god-like task that had before this been only Nature's job, the fashioning of living clay to specific forms, the manipulation of evolution.

Subsequently, using what he had discovered in breeding those early canines for the hunt, mankind shaped the evolution, to some extent, of other beasts when the time came for him to quit being a hunter and enter into the pastoral age. Again he selected and bred his canine companions toward specific purpose, this time as herding canines. And as time passed and man became a social animal and built his cities and monuments, altars to his growing ego, he fashioned the dog into all manner of shapes and sizes, to fit whims that it

Basic, primitive, canine type. This animal was Horand v. Grafrath, the first German Shepherd, registered in 1899. Northern breeds, the Norwegian Elkhound, Keeshonden, and like breeds still retain this basic feral wolf-like form.

E.H.HART

From Horand v. Grafrath evolved the modern German Shepherd, a breed of many purposes, the result of intelligent breeding practices combined with strict selection. The dog is Condor v. Sixtberg, SchH. II, a German import owned by the author.

pleased him to indulge in and not through utilitarian necessity. So the many breeds of dogs came into being as man selected from occasional mutations and subsequently bred to maintain the mutant effect.

But man was not satisfied with this hit and miss procedure of procreation. He wanted more specific control over the evolution of the animals under his hand. For from the time that early man first became aware of himself as an entity that curious and unique part of him called the brain, or mentality, probed questioningly at the world around him as he pondered the "what" and "why" of being.

The first interpretations given to natural phenomena by ancient man were mythological. But even in that early time man must have sensed his relationship to all living things on this Earth he trod, and this subconscious semi-awareness led him to diligently seek the

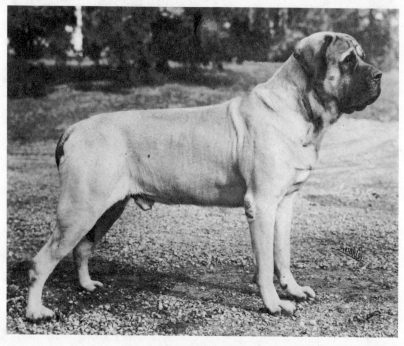

From **Canis familiaris inostranzewi**, through the primitive and ferocious Molossian watch and war dogs, came the modern Mastiff. Close relative to the savage Tibetan Mastiff and the old Bullenbeisser, the Mastiff of today is a huge, handsome, sweet tempered dog of noble mein and type.

The Saluki is a descendent of the prototype dog, Canis familiaris leineri, whose most direct progenitor was the old Egyptian Greyhound. This sight hound is of ancient desert lineage, used by Egyptian and Arab masters to run down the swift desert gazelles and to bring to bay the savage cat creatures that made the desert's edge their habitat.

secrets of life, of reproduction, and of evolution. As early as 500 years before Christ, the Greek philosopher, Thales, applied scientific thought to the subject and shrewdly concluded that all life originated in and came from water (the Aegean Sea). Aristotle, the great Greek philosopher and naturalist, collected and analyzed all facts and zoological data up to his time (384–322 B.C.) and made the first attempt, based on comparative anatomy, to classify the animal kingdom. Jean-Baptiste Lamarck (1744–1829) a French naturalist, recognized the process of evolutionary change, but he theorized that such changes were the result of exposure to various environmental influences and that these environmentally controlled changes were then consigned to the next generation by inheritance. Lamarck's theory persisted for a long time, even in the face of proof to the contrary. As a matter of fact, not too long ago, the leading geneticist in Russia (Lysenko) advanced a similar theory based on the shaping of life-forms through environment rather than heredity. This scientific gentleman was subsequently discredited in the Soviet Union and has since dropped from sight.

So down through the ages men of splendid and inquiring minds used their mentalities, learning, and skills, to shed more light upon the study of specie origin. It remained for one great man to find the key to the origin of species, and that man was, of course, Charles Robert Darwin. He found the answer to the mystery of life in evolution, the theory that all life-forms find kinship through a common and basic ancestry and that divergence occurs to permit variety so that a species can fit into a changing environment. The adaptation of organisms to different environments is accomplished by natural selection. The survival and reproduction of these naturally selected and relatively better adapted individuals brings progressively greater fitness to the species.

Darwin's great book, "The Origin Of Species", and later his famous "The Descent Of Man", resulted in furor throughout the civilized world for it preached the gospel of mankind's relationship to all other animals, and specifically the anthropoids, and denied to man any special, God-given descent. His work brought about tremendous progress in human understanding of life and the world we live in, and it brought hate, ridicule, tumult and religious wrath. Darwin's scientific labor proved the fallacy of biblical Genesis and all things biblical relating to the origin of life on Earth, and so by negating Christian doctrine he caused the battle between science and religion to be joined.

The theory of evolution, as advanced by Charles Darwin, was the first great step forward in man's understanding of inheritance. But to the layman, the farmers who bred meat animals and grew vegetable and fruit foods, to the sportsmen who bred hunting dogs, racing dogs or racing horses, it was not enough to aid them in their endeavors. They were trying to improve their stock and, so far, their only tool was selection. If they wanted to keep and enhance the speed of their Greyhounds they bred the swiftest male to the fastest bitch. Horse breeders followed the same method, and huntsmen selected from litters of puppies for those that most closely resembled their superior gun-dog sires and dams.

The rule of thumb used by the animal breeders was, "Like begets like". Added to this basic prescript was the age-old precept that acquired characters are inherited. The Bible explicitly furthered this deception, specifically in the story of Jacob's experiments in the production of strangely marked sheep. Lamarck's like theories were widely accepted. Acquired characters must be inherited, breeders argued. Therefore it was not enough to breed a hunting dog stud to a hunting dog bitch for the production of good hunting dogs. Since like begets like the progeny will *look* like good hunting dogs, but unless both sire and dam had been hunted in the field they would not be able to pass on to their get the vital ability to become excellent gun dogs, they reasoned.

Those breeders of animals knew that there was something more to heredity. They were not getting true results by application of the only theories they had. Like did not always beget like. True, the results of such breeding were within the borders of breed resemblance. But if like truly could beget like then breeding a top specimen to a top specimen should produce nothing but superb offspring in the image of their parents, and this, of course, just didn't happen. And what of the freaks, the "sports", the odd colors and types that cropped up every so often; where did they come from? How did they fit the theory? Again, if acquired characteristics are inherited, how to explain the great hunting dog that came from parents that had never been hunted in the field, or the stakes-winning race horse, the progeny of a pair of thoroughbreds that had never been raced?

There was something missing, something vital, not yet known or explained, that could give animal breeders much greater ability to control evolution, to mold the beasts they kept for food or fun more surely to their own demands and needs.

Though Darwin did not concur wholly with Lamarck's concept of inheritance, theorizing that evolution occurred by means of natural selection, he nevertheless shared the universal belief that acquired traits were inherited. He advanced a theory which he called a "Provisional hypothesis of pangenesis" to explain the manner in

The theory of the inheritance of acquired characteristics was rather widespread and generally accepted. But biologists and animal breeders sensed that the theory was lacking in some vital aspect, for it did not explain the phenomena of a great hunting dog who was the product of parents that had never been used in the field.

which inheritance might possibly take place. He hypothesized that every part of the body had a diminutive twin of itself to which he gave the name "pangene". Transported by the body blood to the sex glands these "pangenes" united to form the sex cells. As a body part altered or changed an altered "pangene" would be produced, and this "pangene" would produce physical modification in the ensuing progeny.

Darwin was quite well aware that his hypothesis was just an

educated guess and so he stressed its provisional character. But this "pangene" theory, due to Darwin's scientific eminence, sparked thirty years of intense research and experimentation in the field of inheritence. Many biologists, men such as Galton and Weismann, made elaborate and intimate studies on plants and animals to determine if acquired characteristics ever were inherited. The outcome of these controlled, scientific experiments were uniformly negative.

With no true knowledge of the process of inheritance (until Johann Gregor Mendel's theory was given to the world), sportsmen and breeders used the old maxim "like begets like," coupled with selection to breed better race horses and faster Greyhounds.

Scientists, like the breeders of animals, were aware that natural selection produced changes, yet asked how these changes came about. There seemed to be no rules, nothing that could be considered definite, no specific design of endeavor that could be followed to a satisfactory answer. There had to be a pattern of inheritance, but what was it and how did it work?

Darwin, his peers and his followers, were unaware that his basic laws of evolution and the true natural laws of heredity were being

Charles Robert Darwin

developed at approximately the same time. But those all-important laws that would take much of the guess work from breeding, that would be the beginning of a new and tremendously important science, were destined to be tossed aside and hidden from the eyes of man for over thirty years. While men of science strove mightily to find the answers, a man of the cloth in a tiny garden made his experiments, meticulously recorded the results, and found the laws that governed inheritable linkage . . . only to have the results of his studies and his theories almost buried with him. For when he died, Gregor Johann Mendel's great discovery of the true method of inheritance was unknown to the world at large and seemed destined to die with him. The resurrection of his remarkable life's work that answered the baffling questions of his scientific peers, and that gathered dust for over sixteen years after his own death, is perhaps the most dramatic story in the history of scientific endeavor.

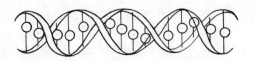

CHAPTER 2

THE RIDDLE OF INHERITANCE SOLVED

In a small but impeccably kept garden behind an Augustinian monastery Gregor Johann Mendel, a Moravian monk, quietly and diligently tended his garden pea plants, watching their growth with an attentive eye. Mendel was an Austrian, born in 1822 in the tiny village of Heinzendorf in Austrian Silesia, a section of Europe which has since become a part of Czechoslovakia. Johann early learned how to improve fruit trees with grafts in his father's orchards and his interest in the growth and development of living things stemmed from that childhood time.

Mendel proved to be a brilliant student in school, avid always for new learning and addicted to the study of nature and her mysteries. His people were poor and Johann, a deeply religious young man, turned to the cloth as the only means available to him to dedicate his life to science and learning and be *"spared perpetual anxiety about a means of livelihood"*. In 1843, accepted in the Augustinian Monastery in Brünn and assuming the name Gregor, he was free, as he continued his religious studies, to work on plant experiments. At first he experimented with flowers and found that when he crossed certain varieties specific characteristics made their appearance regularly. He turned to the breeding of gray and white mice, reading all he could find about hybridization while he amassed data of his own. Nothing published, nothing known to science could help him, he soon found out. Hybridization resulted in a great variety in size, color and form, that seemed to follow no known or given rule.

The studious Monk decided that research in this field had been shallow and without true scientific diligence. He would breed hybrids for generation after generation, recording the changes in characteristics that took place and attempt to find the missing key that would open the door to the evolutionary control of living material. Mendel studiously set down his needs for the great experiment. He decided that he must have a true-breeding legume that could be easily protected from alien pollen and, after testing, he settled upon the common garden pea as the vehicle for his experiments. From 34 original varieties he finally selected 22 species and patiently, thoroughly, he made his breedings by hand pollenization. During the winter months, Mendel worked with the seeds he had extracted from his hybrid plants and gradually his data mounted, data that led to his famous discovery and identification of the units of heredity and the knowledge of how they worked.

Mendel found that when two individual plants which differed in a unit trait were mated, one trait appeared in the subsequent offspring and one did not. The trait which was visible he named the "dominant" trait and labeled this characteristic "A". The character which was not visible he called the "recessive" trait "a". When "A" and "A" came together the result was a pure dominant, or all "A" offspring. When "a" and "a" were mated the result was purely recessive, or "a". Mating "A' to "a" produced the hybrid "Aa" which carried the recessive factor in hidden form ("a"). His crossings of hybrids resulted in the persistent 3 to 1 ratio.

This 3 to 1 ratio had also been found by Charles Darwin in his experiments with hybrids, but he failed to understand the significance of this mathematical fact which was plain to Mendel. The scholarly monk realized that by mating Aa and Aa together he could produce three different combinations, AA, Aa, and aa; with two pairs of hybrids he could get nine genetically different offspring. Compound these three by three by three combinations in cubic power and the possible variations attain an almost impossible-to-grasp number. But there were only six ways in which a single pair of determiners (called by Mendel "units") could combine with a similar pair. The Mendelian expectation chart indicates the expected results of these six uncomplicated genetic combinations. This simple Mendelian law holds true in the actual breeding of all living things—of plants (the monk's experimental vehicle), mice, elephants, fish, humans, or dogs.

Gregor Mendel proposed that all traits, such as outer color for example, are transmitted by units (determiners) in the sex cells and that one of these units must be pure, let us say either black or white, but never a mixture of both colors. From a black parent that is pure

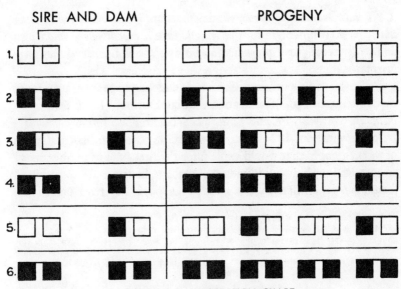

SIRE AND DAM	PROGENY

MENDELIAN EXPECTATION CHART

The six possible ways in which a pair of determiners can unite. Ratios apply to expectancy over large numbers, except in lines no. 1, 2 and 6 where exact expectancy is realized in every litter

for that trait, only black units are transmitted, and from a white parent only white units can be passed on to the progeny. But when one parent is black and the other white a hybrid occurs which transmits both the black and white units in equal amounts. The hybrid itself will exhibit the dominant color (black) but will carry the other color (white) as a recessive (the assumption is that we are dealing with coat color in dogs and that bloth black and white are colors, not absence of color, etc. *See Mendelian Chart*).

Unable to microscopically see these hereditary units, or determiners, that his experiments inexorably proved to exist, the results of his experiments had to be considered theory. But Mendel could, and did, write a forumula for the biological laws that were the substance of his experimental discoveries:

1. The transmission of hereditary factors is accomplished through a large number of independent, inheritable units (or determiners).

2. If each parent contributes an identical factor, a constant character is passed on to the progeny. When each parent furnishes a different factor, the result is a hybrid. In the reproductive cells formed by the hybrid the two different units are again "liberated".

3. *No matter how long the hereditary units are in association with other units, or determiners, in an individual, they are completely unaffected and will emerge from any union as untouched and distinct as they were originally.*

To test his hypotheses Gregor Mendel engaged in two more experiments of cross-fertilization and later wrote, *"In all the experiments there appeared all the forms which the proposed theory demands"*.

In the winter of 1864 Mendel prepared a report on his eight years of work, a paper that would explain for the first time in the history of science and man, how individual characters or traits are transmitted from one generation to the next. This paper he read before the

The fawn color of this Great Dane is the result of a double recessive affecting the genes for color. He is pure for the color fawn, and when bred to a fawn mate can produce nothing but fawn progeny (see **Mendelian chart No. 1**). If bred to a brindle bitch, all the young will be brindle, unless the bitch is carrying a hidden recessive for the fawn color.

Brindle is dominant to fawn, therefore this brindle dog will produce only brindle whelps when bred to a fawn bitch. But, since fawn is recessive, a brindle can carry the fawn color and produce 50% fawn progeny when bred to fawn (see Mendelian Expectation chart No. 5).

Brünn Society for the Study of Natural Science during the course of two meetings. Totally contrary to the then accepted theory of blood as the vehicle of heredity, the small group were completely bewildered by the monk's combination of mathematics and botany and his talk of the strange unseen, internal movement of unknown "units". Mendel's monograph, *"Experiments in Plant Hybridization"*, appeared in the Society's limited publication in 1866, and copies eventually arrived at all the scientific organizations and universities in Europe and America . . . and the learned monk's theory was greeted with thundering silence. No one seemed to give his eight years of work and research any attention at all.

But, undiscouraged, Mendel continued his experiments, this time with hawkweed and then with beans. He eventually discovered another basic law of heredity; that more than one of his units of heredity influenced certain traits. With this finding Mendel had discovered the whole basic pattern of the laws of heredity, the answers to all the questions mankind had asked for centuries.

Galton, a contemporary of Mendel, made an extensive study of coat color inheritance in the Basset Hound. His findings were similar in scope to Mendel's.

On January 6, 1884, Gregor Johann Mendel, by then Abbot of the Monastery, died, just two years after the death of Charles Darwin. In contrast to the acclaim accorded to Darwin during his life and after his death, no one noticed the passing of this great scientist whose tremendous contribution to man's knowledge would eventually bring him immortality. Indeed even the notes and records he had kept of his amazing experiments disappeared.

It must be mentioned here that other scientists, during the time that Mendel was making his experiments and later, were slowly moving toward the same goal as the monk achieved but with different genetic material. Knight, an earlier experimenter in the field, also used garden peas and found results similar, in some respects, to Mendel's. Galton, an English contemporary of Mendel, made an interesting study of coat color inheritance in the Basset Hound, and Hugo de Vries, a botanist at the University of Amsterdam, using Darwin's provisional hypothesis of pangenesis as a base, found that decided changes in some aspects of inheritable material occurred, and he labelled these completely different and unexpected transmissable

Gregor Johann Mendel

traits *"mutations"* (Darwin had noted such changes also and called the carriers *"sports"*).

For a decade De Vries raised or studied 53,509 primrose plants, and through his amassed and tremendous data concluded that characters had to be produced by separate units of heredity which could effect and cause variation in each part separately. The botanist searched diligently through every bit of written material he could find for parallel research and finally, in a work on plant hybridization written by W. O. Focke, a German scientist, he found reference to the work of Gregor Johann Mendel. De Vries sensed at once the importance of this mention and began to avidly seek out more of the work of the Moravian monk and at last, in 1900, discovered the paper Mendel had published in 1866. De Vries knew then that this unknown monk, Mendel, and not he, De Vries, had first solved the ancient riddle of inheritance.

Strangely enough, after all those years of gathering dust, of being completely and thoroughly ignored by the world, Mendel's great work was discovered again almost simultaneously by not just De Vries, but also by a German and an Austrian scientist as well. Their joint confirmation of the great work of Mendel caught the attention of the scientific world and man gained his first true understanding of the greatest of life's mysteries. The name of Gregor Johann Mendel, and the theory of inheritance to which he gave that name, became immortal. Darwin's theory of evolution had at last been given its foundation, and a new science had been born called, genetics.

Golden Retriever

Komondor

Dark brown in coat, with a stub tail, short legs, small round ears, and hyena-like, the South American Bush Dog (Icticyon venaticus) of Brazil, is a very primitive type of wild canine. There are four varieties of this odd creature and a fifth variety that exists in Panama, the latter almost extinct. The Bush Dog weighs about 25 pounds, is badger-like in appearance, vicious, and hunts in packs.

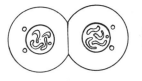

CHAPTER 3

GENES, CHROMOSOMES AND CELLS

Before we delve any deeper into the genetic processes of life and how they can be used by us for breed improvement, we must first clear away the debris of old untruths and superstitions so that we may clearly see the true structure that lies beyond. *The inheritance of acquired characters* is one of the fallacious theories that was widely believed and, I am afraid, has its disciples even today. The Russian agronomist, Lysenko, whom I mentioned earlier, during his ascendancy in the Soviet Union's scientific circles, secured much prestige and power by his attacks on modern genetics and his advocacy of the so-called *"Michurinian"* theory. Lysenko claimed that work done by a fruit-tree breeder, Michurin, made negative the fundamentals of modern biology. When analyzed, this so-called theory was nothing more than reiteration of the earlier Lamarck's belief in the inheritance of acquired characteristics, which Mendel, and the many geneticists who followed him, have proven to be completely without foundation.

Birthmarking is another false theory that must be discarded in the light of present-day genetical knowledge. The genes which give our dogs all their inheritable material are isolated in the body from any environmental influence (exceptions will be mentioned later). What the host does or has done to him or her influences the genes not at all. The so-called "proofs" advanced by the adherents of this bogus theory were simply isolated coincidences.

Telegony, the theory that the sire of one litter could or would influence the progeny of a future litter out of the same bitch but sired by a completely different stud dog, is still another untrue belief and is, in essence, comparable to the foolish concept of *"saturation"*, which postulates that if a bitch is bred many times to the same stud she will become "saturated" with his "blood" and will henceforth be capable only of producing whelps of his type.

Dalmatian

Chinese Crested

By far the most persistent and widely believed theory of inheritance advanced the proposition that the *blood* was the vehicle through which all inheritable material was passed from parents to offspring, from one generation to the next. Though thoroughly discredited the taint of this superstition still persists in the phraseology we employ in our breeding terms such as, *"bloodlines"*, *"percentage of blood"*, *"pure-blooded"*, *"blue-blooded"*, *"new blood"*, etc.

When Mendel's theory, of separate hereditary units accounting for all the different forms of life, became recognized and accepted, it replaced all the other bogus theories such as those discussed at the beginning of this chapter. But acceptance of this new theory led to other questions that needed answers. What *were* Mendel's units, and just *where* were they located in the living body? *How* did they produce these character changes or differences, and was it possible to *control* them? If they could be controlled how was it done, and to what extent could these genetic changes be pushed by man if he *could* control them?

De Vries, Fisher, Haldane and Sewell Wright, all brought their considerable mentalities to bear upon the answers to these questions. Sir Ronald Aylmer Fisher, who later became a professor of genetics at Cambridge, utilized mathematical analysis to discredit De Vries pet theory that mutation was evolution's prime agent. Then, in 1902, W. S. Sutton of Columbia University, suggested that the unseen hereditary units that were the essence of Mendel's theory, might be in the chromosomes. During the years that Mendel's work had been ignored scientists had found diminutive, thread-like substances in the nucleus of all living cells that became manifest under the microscope when dyed. These were the chromosomes, the agents Sutton suggested might be the carriers of Mendel's units.

Sutton was right, but it took many years to verify his guess. Thomas Hunt Morgan, a Nobel prize winner in genetics, and an American biologist, proved through his experiments with common fruit flies (Drosophila melanogaster) that the chromosomes were indeed the physical carriers of Mendel's units of heredity. It took 17 years and the breeding of millions of fruit flies before Morgan and his assistants could map the precise locations, on the four pairs of chromosomes that the fly carried, that controlled specific characteristics. These locations were named genes and, through these remarkable experi-

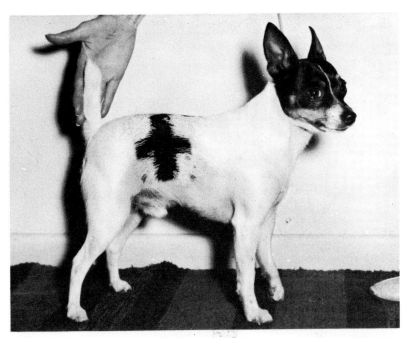

Born on Easter Sunday, the markings on its side forming a distinct cross, this dog could be used as living "proof" of the false theory of birthmarking by advocates of that ridiculous concept.

Fruit flies (**Drosophila melanogaster**), used as vehicles for genetic study by Thomas Hunt Morgan, earned the great geneticist a Nobel prize.

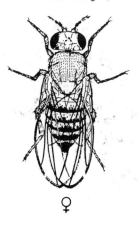

♀

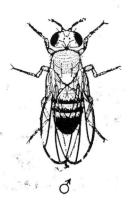

♂

Borzoi

Pomeranian

Bull Terrier

ments and the happy use of fruit flies as study vehicles, Thomas Hunt Morgan became the father of modern genetics.

Other scientists added to the fund of knowledge being amassed, notably Sir Julian Huxley and H. J. Muller. The latter geneticist, also a Nobel prize winner, subjected fruit flies to several forms of radiation, including X-rays, and created a host of mutations by damaging the genes of the insects with this radiation.

Now many of the questions could be answered, particularly those that had been asked by breeders of livestock. The whole plan of inheritance could be shown, like a blue print, to those who wished to view it. Since this is a book about dog breeding let us use a dog as our model and see how this whole affair works.

A dog is made of organs, which are fashioned of tissues, which in turn are made of cells. Each cell contains a specific number of chromosomes. In the fruit fly we have seen that the experimenters found only four pairs of chromosomes in each cell. In the dog there are thirty-nine pairs or seventy-eight chromosomes, thirty-two more than there are in man. We generally speak of chromosomes in pairs because every dog receives half his chromosomes from one of his parents, thirty-nine from his sire and thirty-nine from his dam, and these chromosomes pair off, each one microscopically different from its mate, but appearing to be alike, yet differing from the partners of the next pair.★

Inside the chromosomes are the genes, Mendel's units of heredity, and each gene has a particular location, or "locus", within the chromosome. The number of genes possessed by the dog on each of its chromosomes is not yet known, but it would be a fantastic number since it has been estimated that the fruit fly, with only four pairs of chromosomes, could carry from five to fifteen thousand genes.

★ Author's note: Though there has been little experience in the canine species with the phenomenon of triple chromosomes (probably lethal in dogs) it should be mentioned. Triple chromosomes are due to chromatic change and the influenced individual is genetically labelled a triploid, signifying triple, as diploid implies influence by the usual double chromosomes, and tetraploidy a four chromosome influence, etc. An individual can sometimes have either too few chromosomes (anenploidy) or too many (polyploidy), and in either case the effect can be (but not necessarily) lethal. Of the two known polyploidy types, allopolyploidy and auto-polyploidy, the former is the result of hybrid duplication and can readily change a species or produce a new species in one generation. Polyploidy results in larger, more vigorous individuals with a general exaggeration in structure and parts, and a need by the polyploid for environment that differs from that of the species norm.

The genes packaged in any specific chromosome are linked and will be passed on to the next generation as a unit. This unit of genes that will be issued to the dog's progeny do not effect any one segregate part of the animal; in other words, one package of genes does not

Chromosomes in
nucleus of cell

Chromosomes arranged in
pairs, showing partnership

contain all the elements that effect the animal's tail, let us say. This one gene group could effect every part of the body and the mentality as well.

The chromosomes we have seen, are paired and resemble long, twin strings of beads. But there is an exception to this concept, for one of the thirty-nine pairs is unique . . . the sex chromosome. The female pair is exact and we designate this pair as XX. In the male there is also an X chromosome, but its partner is a Y chromosome.

The genes are also paired, so that a gene that affects some specific characteristic will have a mate affecting the same characteristic and will be in the same position on the paired chromosome. When both these genes are identical the animal is genetically homozygous for that tiny but specific gene influence. If they are different, then the dog is heterozygous for that trait or for that part of a trait. A gene can be dominant or it can be recessive. A gene pair which are different are called "alleles". The dominant allele affects the dog's appearance while the recessive allele is carried unseen in the germplasm. A group of alleles that affect a specific characteristic is called an "allelomorphic series".

The body cells, all of which carry a complete set of chromosomes and genes (Mendel's units), multiply to produce growth or to replace dying cells. The process used by these cells to multiply is called "mitosis" or dividing. Each cell splits apart and becomes two cells, identical in all ways, each twin cell having a complete complement,

Gordon Setter

Fox Terrier

Lhasa Apso

Mitosis beginning. The chromosomes are becoming thicker and more obvious in the nucleus of the cell.

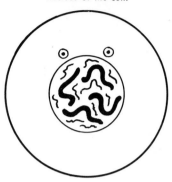

The spindle, which has been forming, now covers the middle of the cell. The nucleus has disappeared and the centrioles (cores of the asters) have divided into separate pairs. The chromosomes have split and will separate and move along the spindle to opposite sides of the cell as the cell prepares to divide.

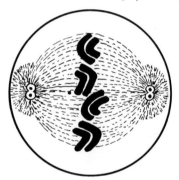

The cell is about to complete division and become two cells. The spindle has vanished, its job done. A nucleus appears in each of the cells in which there now is a complete set of chromosomes and two centrioles (for each cell). Each cell is now complete and perfect in itself, capable, and soon ready, to divide again.

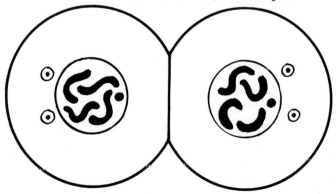

or set, of chromosomes. The body cells in which this occurs are called the "somatic" cells to differentiate them from the sex cells in which a different process takes place. There, in the sex cells, when division takes place, only *half* of the chromosomes (and their genes) are received by each sperm (in the male) or each egg (in the female).*

When mitosis occurs an elaborate mechanism begins to function in the splitting cell that divides and separates the chromosomes, which become very prominent in the cell nucleus in the first stage of division. The chromosomes begin to thicken as they absorb chemicals from the cell, and a spindle (a web of fibers) begins to grow across the cell from a pair of asters (star-shaped substances). As the chromosomes begin their process of exact duplication by splitting lengthwise, the number of fibers in the spindle increases and the wall of the cell nucleus begins to break down to allow the chromosomes to move to opposite ends of the cell. The chromosomes then align themselves in pairs and become attached to the spindle, the fibers of which have spread evenly across the face of the cell to form a ladder on which the chromosomes can climb. At this point in the process of mitosis the nucleus of the cell has completely disappeared and the asters (centrioles) have, in turn, divided into two separate pairs on opposite sides of the cell, with the spread spindle and migrating chromosomes between.

The stage of actual cell division now begins. The chromosomes, which formerly have split to make an exact pairing in the cell, migrate along the spindle fibers to the edges of the cell, each identical pair facing each other but at opposite ends of the cell. The cell itself pinches in at the middle as it begins to divide and the spindle, having performed its function as a ladder for the chromosomes, begins to disintegrate and finally vanishes completely. The cell division continues as a new nucleus forms in each section of the splitting cell and, as mitosis is completed, two cells exist instead of just one, each with its own nucleus, each with its own complete and twin set of chromosomes, and its two sets of centrioles.

In the sex cells of the dog and bitch a "reduction" division occurs, and at a specific stage of division each male spermatozoon and each

---

* Author's note: All living things possess the same genetic attributes so that what you read here can be applied to other hobby animals, but this very important difference must be noted. In mammals the male sex chromosome pair are XY, the female pair XX. In birds, fish, insects, the opposite is true. The male chromosome is XX and the female, XY.

Great Pyrenees

Doberman Pinscher

female ovum (gamete) receives one twin of each pair of chromosomes for transmission to the progeny. Selection of these chromosomes is random. But when the single group of chromosomes carried by the spermatozoa unites with the single group carried by the female egg during the process of breeding, the two groups pair and the embryo that develops in the egg has its full complement of paired chromosomes, one group from each parent.

If the male X chromosome unites with the female X chromosome then the resulting puppy will be a female. But if the male Y chromosome is carried by the particular sperm that fertilizes the female egg, the resulting progeny will be a male (XY). It is, therefore, a matter of chance as to what sex the offspring of any mating will be, since sperm is capricious and fertilization is random.

This splitting of chromatic pairing that occurs in the sex cells (called "meiosis"), is what gives us the very necessary recombinations of chromosomes, and the genes they carry, to produce change or evolution. Each time a male sperm and a female egg unite in reproduction they produce a genetically unique individual, different from its parents, different from its litter mates. Only through this continuous scrambling of genes to produce new individuals can there be a selection of living types available for testing in the crucial flames of evolution for survival choice.

These sex cells also carry sex-linked characters. In the dog not too many of these traits have been recognized. But because they can be hidden by the obvious factors of sex they can sometimes be less than a virtue. An example of how a sex-linked trait in dogs would work is orchidism, or the lacking of one (monorchidism) or two (cryptorchidism) testicles, which have failed to descend into the scrotum. This trait has been labelled genetically as a fairly simple recessive and, as such, must be carried by both sire and dam to be passed on to the offspring. Obviously a female carrying this trait would not show it. But she would pass it on to her young, and if her mate carried the same trait the males in the litter would be obviously affected. So would their female litter mates but, like the dam, in them it would remain physically invisible.

There are more sex-linked factors carried on the X chromosome than on the Y. Of course here there is no necessity for the gene to have an opposing allele for in the male there is no paired X to carry the opposing factor. A recessive characteristic carried on an X

In any mating the sex of the resulting offspring is a matter of chance. But each puppy is a genetically unique individual, never exactly like its litter brothers or sisters, or any individual ever produced in the breed.

chromosome would, in the male, become manifest, and this X chromosome would have come to him from his dam. This explains how congential afflictions can be hosted (or carried) by the female but only affect the male (her sons). In humans hemophilia and a particular type of color blindness are examples of such sex-linked diseases.

If we can visualize this distribution of traits that occur from each breeding as a game of cards perhaps what happens can be even more clearly explained. Sex is the dealer who shuffles the deck and deals the hands. Each deal represents a new breeding, each shuffle a mixing of all the cards (the chromosomes), and each hand the random joining of cards. Every matching pair in the hand represents a fully dominant or fully recessive trait, or part of a trait (homozygous). If there are no pairs the hand is heterozygous. The odds of receiving the same hand twice is, as you know, tremendous. As a matter of fact the odds against the joining of a specific combination of two sets of exactly designed chromosomes in a bitch's fertilized egg would be approximately two million to one.

So far we have considered the chromosomes and the cells. Now let us examine the genes, those tiny bits of living material that dictate

Papillon

Labrador Retriever

A bitch, no matter how lovely in type, can carry the taint of orchidism and pass it on to her male progeny. Being female she will not exhibit the fault herself, but her male puppies obviously will.

the all of life. That they are chemically constituted has been scientifically established and great advances in genetics were achieved when the science was approached from the chemical angle. In 1940, a new and genuinely pliable genetic material was found in Neurospora crassa, a mold, which replaced the fruit fly as a vehicle for experimentation.*

We have seen how a bombardment of X-ray radiation produced a host of mutations in the fruit fly by changing or distorting the genes, but generally speaking the genes are securely insulated from outside influence. Environment can affect an individual but not its germ plasm. For instance, if a puppy's nutritional needs are not fully provided for during its most intense period of growth, its end potential will not be obtained upon maturity. It will lack size and substance, show evidence of rickets, etc. But regardless of its outward appearance, the animal's germ plasm, its inheritable material, remains inviolate and capable of passing on to the next generation the potential that was denied the dog itself by improper feeding.

The exact chemistry of the gene was a secret until a brilliant series of experiments at the Biological Laboratory, Cold Springs Harbor, unlocked the door to a vital new aspect of inheritance. It was known that the genes contained chemical messages that were given to and controlled the metabolism, the growth and reproduction of the cell. A living cell is contantly in the throes of chemical change. The genes, combined with other chemical regulators in the cell called enzymes, control the rate of speed and the sequence of these chemical changes. In other words they, the genes, act as chemical regulators and, in this capacity, control the development of the organism in which they reside.

Genes can, and do, mutate. Mutation is the sudden appearance of an unexpected hereditary trait that is alien to the hereditary design of the species or family. An obvious example would be a Great Dane or a German Shepherd dog, or any individual from a long-tailed breed, being born with a natural short, or possibly a screw tail. Mutations can be caused by the loss of a gene or the gain of a gene, or a change in a gene. Many more gene mutations actually take place than were formerly suspected, but most of the changes are either

---

* Author's note: Molds produce a new generation every 10 days as do fruit flies. A virus reproduces every 20 minutes! It is no wonder that geneticists have now turned to the use of viruses for study. The viruses utilized for this purpose are grown on chicken or monkey cells.

Viszla

Great Dane

Flat-coated Retriever

Mutations change the expected genetic design of the affected individual. Obvious, visible change by mutation can be easily evaluated and selected for or against by the breeder. Mutation adds variety to genetic material.

hidden within the body of the dog, or affect recessive genes and are thus invisible. The dramatic mutations which affect the physical surface, such as the one used as an example above, are those we notice and select for or against according to whether they direct us toward our breeding goal or not. Again, with the vagary inherent in all living matter, a mutated gene can change back to its original form or mutate to a further degree or in another direction.*

Mutation maintains the stock of genetic variance at a high level, and makes it possible for a species to adapt to new conditions instead of becoming a victim to environmental change with which it cannot cope. It is true that most mutations are detrimental, as would any change in a breed that had almost reached perfection. Some mutations are even lethal. But a very minute change or mutation might not even be noticed and could, in the long run, prove to be beneficial if,

* Author's note: There are four factors which cause change by breaking genetic equilibrium: Mutation; Selection; Migration; Genetic drift. In our controlled breeding of dogs we are concerned only with the first two factors, not with the last two which can be replaced by a single factor pertinent to our breeding practices, namely, environment.

Many mutational variations are not visible and exist hidden within the animal. Mutation is sometimes harmful to the host and sometimes not. The sire and dam can carry mutational variation that the English Cocker puppy above inherited in a hidden, recessive state.

at some time in the future, the standard of the breed was changed.

Mutation keeps the gene-pool from becoming stagnant and, in so doing, becomes the fountainhead of evolution. Each generation adds variety to inheritable material through mutation. Mendelian re-combination coupled with sexual reproduction bring the mutant genes into new combinations, and natural selection tests these variances and either keeps or discards them. It is interesting to note that in the fruit fly about one quarter of all genetic mutations are either lethal or semi-lethal. Sterility is produced in one or both of the sexes in approximately fifteen to twenty percent of all mutations affecting Drosophila melanogaster. There is a varied reduction in vitality and vigor displayed by many mutants. Mutations that are induced by radiation, drugs or poisons, are almost invariably harmful to the host. Mutations that occur spontaneously from natural causes are not, as we have seen, *necessarily* harmful and can, in the long run, be beneficial.

Occasionally, just before the chromosomes divide in the sex cells, there can occur a process called crossing-over, caused by a quick and

Afghan Hound

Poodle

intimate twisting together of the opposing members of the chromosome pairs. This movement allows genes to relocate on a different chromosome. As a result there will be a changed correlation of genetic characters in the chromatic gene packet which will be passed on intact to the progeny. If, for instance, a breeder of Wire Fox Terriers was getting splendidly long heads in his stock with nice long necks and, worse luck, a correspondingly longer-than-wanted back, this could mean that the long head and neck might not be necessarily transmitted (after the crossing over) with the long back and, instead, the breeder would get a shorter back than ever before. This is just an easily understood example, for the head, neck, and back of any canine could only be formed as a result of the intereaction of a multitude of genetic factors. Crossing-over can cause a distinct variance in the expected genetic picture since, like mutation, it changes Mendelian balance.

Another factor that can have the same effect is epistasy, which is the covering or concealing of one genetic character by another. An epistatic factor acts like a dominant in that it suppresses another factor or factors and, in so doing, can conceal a dominant in an individual so that the breeder will not know it is there. A dominant, of course, makes itself visible at the expense of its opposing, recessive gene, but an epistatic factor superimposes its effect upon an allele (gene) that is located somewhere else on the chromosome and, in so doing, distorts the normal relationship of the gene pair it affects.

There are various other complications that can occur genetically that can thwart direct application of Mendelian theory or distort expectation at the gene level. Environment, if hostile inwardly (chemically) or outwardly, can restrict the full expression of a dog's genetic pattern. In some instances Mendelian dominance can vary in degree and, when this occurs, it is known as partial dominance. Partial dominance seems random in intensity due to the great variation it exhibits in penetration, but is probably affected by many other factors, possibly the sum total of the animal's genetic composition plus environment.

Many paragraphs back I mentioned the work done at Cold Spring Harbor that began the last known step in genetic understanding, and which brings us up to the present day. It had been learned by experimenters previously that a specific nucleic acid existed which could be found only in chromosomes. This whitish powder, when

Another contemporary wild dog is the coyote-like,
Dusicyon culpaeus reisii, commonly called the Equa-
dorian Wild Dog. About the size of a medium to
small dog, they are representative of a group of
South American canines which resemble both dogs
and foxes but are nevertheless true canines. This
type of canine was probably very much a part of
the genetic background of our domestic dog.

Brittany Spaniel

Irish Wolfhound

analyzed, had been found to be different chemically from any other known cellular material. It was subsequently named deoxyribonucleic acid and designated DNA for easier recognition. Shortly afterward another similar nucleic acid was found that seemed to be quite similar to DNA, and it was named RNA (ribonucleic acid). Both DNA and RNA put amino acids together to make proteins. And, most important of all, they are capable of making exact copies of themselves with more proteins, constantly reproducing themselves, a process of startling uniqueness. This is indeed the stuff of which all life is made, the process that produces evolution, the nucleus of heredity, the chemical that genes are made of, the miraculous molecule that is a chemical "Svengali" with complete domination over its "Trilby", all living cells.

DNA is a spiral molecule that has two coils and is linked by four interlocking subunits of chemical composition. The heredity of any life form is determined by the sequence in which these chemical subunits are arranged. RNA acts as the carrier of the inheritable "code" given it by DNA and assembles the correct chemicals to make the

Occasionally the relocation of genes on a different chromosome (crossing over) can prove to be beneficial to the breeder, bringing a correlation of wanted type aspects, such as the long head and short back looked for in the Fox Terrier.

dictated proteins, synthesizes the proteins (aided by electrical forces), and completes the pattern it has received from DNA, which has, through its agent, RNA, directed growth and body chemistry in the cell.*

So tiny it requires an exceptionally powerful electron microscope to be seen, yet so omniscient that it contains within itself a creative diversity that commands uncountable billions of forms; this is DNA composed of four nucleotides which produce twenty universal amino acids, which in turn yield over one hundred thousand proteins that give shape, form and substance to the infinite variety of life forms. DNA exists in all living cells and many scientists postulate that this master chemical of life, DNA, utilizes all living things, including dogs and humans, as vehicles for the constant reproduction of more DNA.

DNA is the last link in the chain of truth forged by the hypothesis of Charles Darwin and Gregor Johann Mendel.

---

* Author's note: Of interest to those engaged in dog training is the improvement affecting both learning and memory in animals by boosting the supply of RNA. A chemical, Cylert (trade name), is fed which increases RNA synthesis twofold or threefold. RNA extracted from the brains of trained animals can accelerate learning, it is now thought, when injected into untrained animals.

Rhodesian Ridgeback

Saluki

Evolved from ancient Roman cattle dogs bred to
native stock, the Rottweiler is the visible manifestation of typical Teutonic thoroughness in the fashioning of a breed to utilitarian purpose.

CHAPTER 4

GENETICS AND THE DOG BREEDER

Except for entertainment value, everything you have read up to now is absolutely useless unless it can be applied by the breeder, in actual breeding practice, to reach an end result. In this chapter, therefore, we will see how genetics can be employed to give the breeder specific results in the whelping box.

To begin we must divorce ourselves from all emotional ties to our animals when we think in terms of breeding. We must see them as living expressions of specific inheritable material. Each bitch that stands before us, each stud dog that we intend to use, each puppy we produce, is not just one dog, but two. Every living thing is a Jekyll and Hyde, shadow and substance. The substance is the dog that lives and breathes and moves in front of us, the animal we see, the physical manifestation of genotypic characters and environment —the *"phenotype"*. The shadow is the dog we don't see; yet this shadow is as much a part of the dog as the animal we see. This shadow-dog is the gene-complex, or total collection of all its genes the *"genotype"*.

The substance, the visible animal, is easily evaluated, but the shadow, the unseen, invisible dog, must also be clearly known and evaluated, for both shadow and substance contribute equally to the reproductive value of the dog and its effect on the generations to come. Without understanding as much as we can of the genetic picture (both shadow and substance) of any particular dog we cannot hope to successfully use that animal to accomplish improvement or any specific results. To acquire this necessary knowledge we must delve into the genetic background of the animal's ancestry, weigh what we find against the producing ability of the dog, check the animal out like a genetic detective, until the shadow becomes as clearly discernible (within reason) as the substance and we can

Bedlington Terrier

Australian Terrier

evaluate the dog's genetic worth as a whole and know him for what he is; the containing vessel, the custodian, of a specific pattern of heredity that we can mold toward envisioned results.

Every dog of any breed is, genetically, unique (with the possible exception of identical twins). The possibility that any two dogs, now living or having lived, could have identical sets of genetic material is just about zero. Every canine has a hereditary endowment which is completely exclusive to itself, unprecedented in the ages past, and not liable to be duplicated in the future. But the breeder of fine dogs today does not face a completely heterozygous maze of unknown genetic heritage. Man has been breeding dogs for some seven thousand years, has selected for various attributes which he desired, and fashioned the fantastic number of breeds we have at the present time. The breeder, therefore, works within a definite sphere of reference; his own particular breed. This means that he or she works with inheritable material that has already been molded to certain specifications, for uncountable blocks of genes have been balanced to constantly reproduce a dog of a certain size, of specific physical characteristics, and displaying a certain kind of temperament. In the long process of fashioning any breed, temperament is important, for a St. Bernard with the temperament of a fiery little terrier would be both dangerous and impossible to live with. By the same token a small terrier as phlegmatic as a big Saint would be boring to have around and not fit to do the job the terrier was originally bred to do.

From a perusal of previous chapters we know now that no breeder can have a definite formula or blueprint for creating the perfect dog, and we, as breeders, are also aware that in our stock there are genetic faults that we wish to eliminate, and yet we wish also to hold the virtues inherent in that stock. Just how do we do this? The answer is, through completely objective study of the dog's ancestors, what they produced, analysis of litter mates, what they produced bred to certain mates, and by test matings of the specific animals you have at your disposal. If you can possibly gather together a three generation picture pedigree it can be of great help in visualizing how a fault is passed down from one generation to the next, and to what degree it is affected by the various breedings in the pedigree.

For what we now know of the random selection of the thirty nine pairs of chromosomes, prior to reduction-division, that line up eventually with the chance set of the mate to produce the full com-

The temperament specific to our various breeds of dogs has been bred in to fit their size and use. A St. Bernard with the character of a Terrier would be a menace, and a Terrier as phlegmatic as a huge Saint would have little appeal and be unable to do the job of "varmint" hunting he was bred for.

Shih Tzu

English Cocker Spaniel

plement of seventy-eight chromosomes, it would seem that the breeder's ability to control any genetic factor would be mathematically impossible. But attempting to control specific characteristics is not by any means futile because, as I mentioned before, we are dealing with a particular breed which has been established (to fit a specific standard) by the same kind of close inbreeding that is at the breeding base of most "pure bred" dogs. This means that during the long decades of the breed's fashioning many of the chromosomes have become homozygous for genetic breed traits. This being so it is easier to chart the correlations of genetic traits that are handed down in the chromosome packets.

Standards have, in many cases, been the result of a timid reach for classical beauty in the specific breed, a group leaning toward artistic expression. Utilitarian purpose, if any, was disregarded, and in any number of cases such purpose was no longer pertinent and could be scorned. But the basis of all breeds was molded by natural evolution for the survival of the animal in the natural state. When the fancier selects for points of "beauty" in a breed that are inimical to survival

Eye color, and coat color, in most breeds, are easy to predict if the genetic formula of the parents in these specific areas is known, and the Menedelian Expectation chart is employed. Dark eyes are dominant, but the fawn Boxer in our illustration can have a slightly lighter eye than the deep brindle dog without it being as obvious because of the difference in coat color.

The shoulder assembly of any dog is the result of a complex genetic design that cannot be changed or altered in one or two breedings. The blue merle coat of this Collie is the result of a dilution factor and can be carried by both sable and tri-colored dogs recessively.

under natural conditions he will find that it is difficult to establish the wanted characteristics and, once established, hard to hold.

There are some few traits, such as eye color, that are determined by simple Mendelian dominant and recessive alleles. A light eye is recessive to a dark eye, so it is easy to get dark eyed progeny in one generation by following the Mendelian Expectation Chart in the previous chapter. Remember that dominant and recessive traits are fashioned by nature, not by man, and they will always remain dominant or recessive. Traits that are "natural", that fit nature's basic pattern for the canine race, are dominant. Those that are not natural, that have been selected by man from mutations and departures from the norm, are generally recessive. Remember, though, that recessives can be "pure" and be visible just as are dominants, but the recessives must be paired for the visible trait.

Many (or perhaps I should say, most) genetic factors, as we

Affenpinscher

Samoyed

recognize them and see the need for some correction in the dog, are the result of complicated inheritance. As an example, let us say that you have a fine bitch that has less than the 90 degree shoulder angulation that the standard of this particular breed calls for. In other words, she has a fairly steep shoulder. By checking both her basic breed type and all her close ancestors, etc. we come to the conclusion that this steeper shoulder that she possesses is dominant (because it is closer to basic canine type than the more angulated shoulder). The shoulder consists of the scapula, or shoulder blade, and the humerus, or upper arm, and these two bones connect to form the degree of angulation in the shoulder. To simplify matters in this example, we will disregard the muscles and ligaments that hold the bones in place and cause them to be activated when a command, sent by the animal's brain, dictates movement.

Let us also assume that this bitch does not move correctly in front because of this lack of angulation called for by the breed standard. She cannot reach forward to balance the thrust from her well-angulated hindquarters and therefore "falls into her forehand" when moving. To get the wanted shoulder it will be necessary to produce a double recessive in the bitch's progeny and then breed to hold the recessives pure in subsequent generations. Knowing how complicated inheritance is you will not attempt to bring recessive perfection to the whole shoulder assembly at once. Instead you will recognize the fact that by getting the proper length and angulation in the humerus, or upper arm, half of your problem will be solved and besides, the necessary reach while moving will come with the correct upper arm layback. The reason you will breed to correct just this one bone is because it is much easier to attempt to make small advances in the wanted genetic direction than to try to change an assembly of compli-cated genetic traits.

You will check your bitch's breeding, and survey get she has had from previous breedings, if any, in an attempt to determine if she may be carrying recessives for the more correct layback of the upper arm. If she isn't, then she is purely dominant for the trait and you will not visibly improve it in her progeny. The only way you can expect improvement is to breed her to a stud who possesses the long, angulated upper arm as a pure recessive. If you can establish this then you know that through this mating, though the progeny will all exhibit the dominant, fairly straight and short upper arm of the dam, they will also carry the recessive longer, better angulated humerus of the sire (see #2, Mendelian Expectation Chart).

As Mendel noted, there are six ways in which his "units" could unite and, by using the expectation chart, the breeder can get a workable idea of what he can expect from specific matings. Simply designate the black areas as dominants and the white areas recessives.

How do you, when you analyse the animal's forebears and pedigree, litter mates, etc., know which are dominant traits and which recessive? By checking out your findings against the following rules which are known to govern the genetic activity of both dominant and recessive characters. We can be reasonably sure that a dominant trait:

1. Does not skip a generation.

2. Will affect a relatively large number of the progeny.

3. Will be carried only by affected individuals.

4. Will minimize the danger of continuing undesirable characteristics in the strain.

5. Will make the breeding formula of each individual quite certain.

With recessive traits we note that:

1. The trait may skip one or more generations.

2. On the average a relatively small percentage of the individuals in the strain carry the trait.

3. Only those individuals which carry a pair of determiners for the trait, exhibit it.

4. Individuals carrying only one determiner can be ascertained only by mating.

5. The trait must come down to the individual from both sire and dam.

With this knowledge of the rules that apply to dominant and recessive traits you can, with a little diligent genetic detective work, gradually bring that shadow-dog into sharper focus. We should not consider this shadow-dog, the genotype, separately from the phenotype, for they are one genetically, they merge, they form a unified continuum, related each to the other in a harmonic structure.

It is obvious by now that, without sharp study, one cannot tell the breeding potential of any animal. It is also clear that conformational corrections cannot be made with any hope of great success in one generation. The odds of the proper recombination of genetic material from one breeding is astronomical. It is necessary then, to begin your breeding activities with animals that are as close to being

Whippet

Pug

Both sire and dam give equally to their progeny of their genetic heritage. If one proves to be more prepotent than the partner, for better or worse, it indicates that that particular animal has been endowed with more dominant genetic characteristics than its mate.

models of the breed ideal as possible, for the less you have to change the more certain you can be of success. It is necessary too, once you have achieved change in the wanted direction, to keep it as a constant in your stock. And this can only be done when you know definitely how you originally brought about the change genetically.

Do not expect to find exact genetic ratios in regard to the uniting of determiners. Such ratios are only exact when there is a union between two dominants, two recessives, or a dominant and a recessive. Even a fertile bitch bred every season and producing a multitude of off-spring until late in her life, will not give you exact Mendelian ratio in the remaining three ways in which the Mendelian Expectation Chart tells us it is possible for determiners to unite. The ratios were established over hundreds of like breedings.

You will hear breeders say that the bitch contributes 60 percent or more to the heredity of the puppies. Others swear that the influence of the sire is greater than that of the dam. We know that neither is correct, for we have seen how each puppy receives 50 percent of its germ plasm from each parent. If one parent is more dominant (or carries more dominant genes) than the other, it may seem as though the puppy has received most of its inheritable material from that parent because the dominant genetic characters will be visible. But the fact remains that the puppy will be carrying just as much of the other parent's genetic contribution in a hidden, or recessive state. Some of these recessives that we can't see may be just as, or perhaps more, important to us in breeding toward an ideal as the dominants we see, and it behooves us to be aware of them so that we can, through clever breeding, match them and bring them to the surface.

From the fact that the puppy's parents also both received but one set of chromosomes from each of their parents and in turn have passed on but one of their sets to the puppy, it would seem that one of those sets that the grandparents contributed has been lost and therefore the whelp has inherited the germ plasm from only two of its grandparents, not four. But we know that selection of inherited traits in the sex cells is random, and it is possible for the youngster's four grandparents to have each contributed an equal 25 percent of all the genes inherited, or various and individual percentages, one grandparent contributing more and another less. It is even possible for the pup to inherit no genetic qualities at all from one grandparent and 50 percent of all its genes from another. Remember, too, that

Chow Chow

Irish Setter

each puppy in a litter has, in all probability, inherited a different proportion of inheritable material from the grandparents. Statistical average is seldom correct when dealing with material so lacking in stability.

One of the indisputable facts that begins to emerge from any study of inheritance is that the chance of arriving at a specific and wanted genetic design is greatly enhanced by sheer numbers. It behooves the breeder, therefore, to make as many breedings and produce as many litters as possible. If the breeder salvages one very fine pup out of every twenty which he raises during a year, then the knowledgable breeder who raises forty pups a year doubles his ability to produce a superb specimen. The more puppies you breed the better statistical chance you have of getting a few better dogs. So most geneticists argue, and genetically we cannot refute this statement.

But there are other considerations which, in the long run, make the odds for multitudinous production nil. The more breedings made to produce the one animal who exhibits a happy combination of genetic virtues, the more ordinary animals that are produced, sold, and used for breeding. Eventually your breed, as a whole, will be downgraded to mediocrity. Assembly-line breeding may be scientific but it eliminates the individual's deep absorption in breeding as a hobby, and entirely disregards the aesthetic connotation inherent in the production of a thing of living beauty fashioned through the efforts of the individual.

Numerical production of this kind also leads to slip-shod methods and a dependence upon sheer numbers alone to reach the desired results. But the individual who has one, two, or a limited number of bitches for breeding cannot afford to miscalculate with any breeding made. Such a breeder is very careful in his selection of breeding partners and is the type of individual who will buy and read this book and plan all his breedings to ensure genetic improvement toward the ideal in his stock.

Plan your breedings on paper, using the knowledge you will gain from this book as a guide to genetic interpretation. Take into consideration both the animal and what it mirrors genetically, and be content with small advances, within the genetic design of your animals, toward your goal. Be constantly alert to recognize any mutation for betterment, that one-in-a-million occurrence, and hold it by crossing back to the unique mutant dog that exhibits the dramatic change.

Weigh everything that is to be put into each breeding by the two dogs involved on the scale of genetic knowledge, so that you can make quite an accurate chart of the genetic makeup of all your dogs, and so that you will be able to chart future proposed breedings.

Remember that recessives can be carried in the chromosomes for generation after generation, often since the time of the breed's beginning, and not be manifest until they meet a like recessive in a specific mating. Such recessives can be the cause of long coated puppies appearing in short coated breed litters (such as in German Shepherds, Weimaraners, etc.), or solid white pups in litters of color-coated dogs (the "Checks", or white pups that appear in Boxer litters).

Some dominants are not decisive in genetic affect and display instead, varying penetrance, or uneven dominance; and additive

Working with a limited number of breeding animals brings more satisfaction in its wake than indulging in numerical production. The color of the Weimaraner was achieved mostly through selection from Red Schweissehund stock that had been affected by the **Isabellismus** factor; combined recessives for dilution that change the base coloration.

Black and Tan Coonhound

Belgian Sheepdog

effects are generally attributed to the influence, on a homozygous level, of several pairs of "multiple factor" genes. Occasionally certain gene combinations prove to be lethal or semi-lethal to their host. Some types of white coat color, for instance, bring genetic deafness in their wake. Most of these latterly mentioned genetic defects the breeder should be aware of but need not consider to any great extent in practical dog breeding. But they should not be forgotten since genetic ills can be motivated by such factors. Hip dysplasia (also known as "subluxation"), a defect which is afflicting many breeds today, has its roots in genetic factors. One authority claims that this anomaly is the result of a partial dominant factor that varies in its degree of penetrance. One of the vital jobs of the breeder is to be sure that, when selecting to genetically "fix" a cosmetic virtue, he does not, at the same time, intensify or unite correlating factors (existing on the same chromatic packet) that will bring into affect lethal, defective, or abnormal factors. Generally such genetic ills can only be made obvious by test breeding.

To assure the holding of any genetic virtue, cosmetic or otherwise, the breeder must assess the factors from the standpoint of "pedigree", or "breeding depth". In other words, thoroughly search the background of the individual if, in breeding, you wish to keep stable any specific virtue, to determine how many generations of forebears behind the animal also had this same virtue. If the dog's sire and dam, and the grandparent's display this same quality, there is a good chance that it has been stabilized in your dog and it carries the virtue in either a purely dominant or a purely recessive state. Studies in "pedigree depth" have proven valuable in controlling hip dysplasia. Recovery of usable progeny from dysplastic animals averaged about 6 percent only, in one study, but when breedings were made from sound dogs whose parents were also free of the disease, the percentage of normal puppies reached over 70. Further experimentation indicates that more than 90 percent of free-from-dysplasia whelps can be expected from parents that show sound stock behind them for two or more generations.

After millions of years of evolution man, for the last few thousand years, has taken over the evolution of most of the canine species and has learned, through the study and theory and brilliant mental work of learned men, how best to control the evolution of the dog, even as you will have learned, through perusal of this book, how best to

Inherited physical anomalies or diseases such as hip dysplasia, which today plagues so many fine breeds, can make negative all of the earnest breeder's efforts. This is particularly true of working or sporting dogs like this black Labrador Retriever whose genetic heritage can be obviated by physical disability.

Bouvier des Flandres

Keeshond

The dog, like all other animals, must adapt to change through mutation or the linkage of recessive characteristics not previously needed but carried, nevertheless, in the animal's genetic formula. The Bloodhound, of ancient and basic hound type, has survived due to its extraordinary olfactory senses.

use the tools those scientists have given us. This is all you need to know. More would confuse and take the zest from your hobby without adding anything constructive. But before we leave the subject, one more important phase must be examined: the relationship of animal to man in regard to genetics.

Though man is an animal and follows the pattern of genetic inheritance precisely as the lower animals do, we must not fashion a parallel between the two. Animals have only biological heredity, while man is greatly influenced by a very complicated and demanding cultural or social inheritance. In our breeding operations with animals we can select, but man does not, and the mesh of civilization which he has woven around himself does not allow for natural selection except in extreme cases. Though social inheritance is not transmitted through the chromosomes and genes, being an acquired characteristic, it is nevertheless linked with inheritance in that it is absorbed by the reasoning human brain. In this factor lies the great difference between man and animal. Man can reason and invent, the animal cannot. Man conquers environment through imagination, reason, and invention; the animal either adapts to change through mutation, genetic changes in structure and function, or it dies.

The study of genetics continues unabated. What we know today is of immeasurable importance in animal breeding, removing a great deal of the guesswork of the past from our operations. Today, by genetic charting and knowledge of inheritable factors, dairymen can produce cows guaranteed to give a specific amount of milk and a definite measure of cream. Farmers can produce hogs from boars that are guaranteed to show absolute percentages of fat to lean meat. Cattlemen can guarantee that calves from specific bulls will gain a specified amount of weight for every pound of food they eat. I could go on, covering the many fields of animal husbandry, and show you how a knowledge of genetics has advanced the breeding of these animals to a point where many of the wanted virtues can definitely be bred in and the result is no longer guesswork. Because these are food animals and therefore a part of the social-economic picture, the breeders have been given the benefit of highly specialized and intense genetic and scientific programs. Dog breeders have not had such advantages, for dogs are not economically important and the kind of necessary clinical experiments that would give us many of the answers we need have not yet been done.

No, we do not know enough to make the breeding of top stock a cut-and-dried matter, or to reduce it to the realm of pure science, with a definite answer to every problem. And this is where the fascination lies. Life is spontaneous and many times unstable, so that even with the greater genetic knowledge that the future will no doubt bring, it is possible that the breeding of great dogs will still remain a combination of science and art, with a touch of genius and aesthetic innovation as happy necessities.

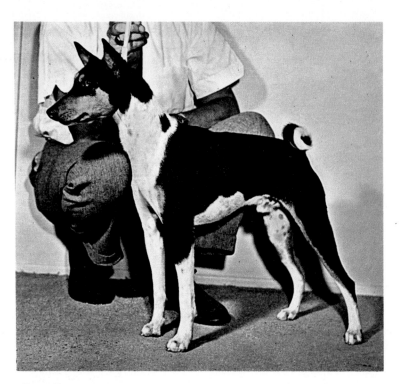

Basenji

Bulldog

One of the strangest of contemporary wild dogs is
the Small-eared Dog of South America (**Atelocynus
microtis**). Also called Sclater's Dog, and the Round-
eared Dog, it is said to be similar in many respects
to prehistoric **Tomarctus**, the prototype canine. It
varies in color from black with a red mask and
pale underbody, to red coat with pied patches of
white or fawn. Weighing about 20 pounds it hunts
small deer, rodents and wild pigs.

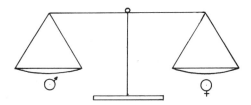

CHAPTER 5

BASIC BREEDING TECHNIQUES

Self expression is a natural need of man. There was a time when people gathered together for good talk, to play chess, to listen to or to play good music. But in today's mechanistic world of rapid pace, specialization, and easy and varied pleasures and entertainment, artistic activity, the ability to express oneself, the creative urge in man, has been all but lost by the throttling environment in which we exist. We who breed dogs are extremely fortunate, for in the process of this facet of our hobby we can give full rein to our inherent and necessary creativeness, to express our needs, our personalities, in living flesh and beauty. Our tools are the units of inheritance, and our art, their infinite combinations. We have the power to create an animate masterpiece if we skillfully use the tools, the breeding techniques, that are ready to our hands, a work of art that will exhibit the evidence of our touch for generations to come.

The breeding techniques that follow have been used with marked success in all forms of economic production and reproduction. They have been tested in the laboratory and in the field. And now that we have absorbed some of the basic facts of heredity we can, with greater understanding, examine the various kinds of breeding that can be used in perpetuating wanted characteristics.

We have learned that within the design of the germ plasm great variation occurs. But within each breed itself as a whole, there is a limit to this variety due to specific breed boundaries. Within each breed boundary there is an average, or norm, which the great majority of the breed mirrors. Draw a straight horizontal line on a piece of paper and label this line, "norm". Above this line draw another and label it, "above norm". This latter line represents the top dogs, the great ones, and the length of this line will be very much shorter than the length of the "norm" line. As a matter of fact it will be quite

Italian Greyhound

Boston Terrier

short. Below the "norm" line draw still another line, designating this to be, "below norm". These are the animals possessing faults which we do not wish to perpetuate, and this line will be longer than the "above norm" line, but shorter than the "norm" mark.

Your breeding objective is with each breeding, or at least each season's breeding, to shorten the "below norm" and lengthen the "above norm" lines. This is the initial step. Once it has become an accomplished fact (within reason), your next objective will be to raise your "below norm" stock up to your present "norm", and your "norm" line to the "above norm" indication. This will establish your top group beyond anything you have yet bred. As time and breeding seasons progress, your stock should improve to such an extent that the dogs which were "above norm" last season would now be only "norm". Select for each season's breeding only those animals which are in the "above norm" bracket, and perhaps one or two of the best, in type and breeding, from the "norm" group.

This method is termed "upgrading", and is basic regardless of what breeding methods you use. The number of breeders who have molded the characteristics of any breed are legion. So many have bred without a basic knowledge of any breeding fundamentals that the stock produced from such haphazard reproduction has the detrimental effect of dangerously lowering the norm. Examine the pedigrees of your dogs and in many instances you will find an example of this—a line incorporated into your pedigree that causes worry to the true student of breeding. Among the other, many objectives of the breeder, nullifying the affect of this weak line must also be on the agenda.

If we are to achieve the greatest good from any program of breeding, there are four important traits which we must examine. It is essential that these characteristics should never be less than normal.

1. *Fertility*. The lack of this essential in any degree must be guarded against diligently.

2. *Vigor*. Loss of vigor, or hardiness, with the coming of its allied ills such as, lowered resistance to disease, finicky eaters, etc., will lead to disaster.

3. *Longevity*. An individual of great breeding worth, who represents a fortunate combination of excellent characteristics which he (or she) dominantly passes on to the progeny, must be useful for a long time after his or her worth is recognized by the progeny produced, so that full opportunity may be taken of the animal's genetic virtues.

Occasionally a fine individual will be produced from a poor family, but inevitably it is useless for breeding for it passes on its negligible genetic heritage to its progeny who exhibit all the faults of the line.

4. *Temperament.* Here is the sum total of the dog's usefulness to man in the various categories in which he serves, from pet to police dog. Lack of true breed character can nullify any physical advances made through your breeding program.

What I have designated as the "norm" can be likened to the force of gravity, possessing a powerful pull toward itself so that regression toward the average is strong, even though you have used parents, in your breeding, that are both above average. The same holds true of animals bred from below "norm" stock, but constant use of such stock will steadily increase the number of below norm animals in your litters and, in the end, lower the standard you have set for your norm. Such animals will seldom produce individuals that will reach the above norm rating. Of course occasionally a dog of superior structure and good enough to reach the above norm qualification is produced by a poor family of generally below norm quality (or lack of quality). Inevitably such an animal is useless for breeding, no matter how superb it may be as an individual, for it will usually

Schnauzer

Bichon Frise

produce in its progeny all its objectionable family traits and none of the fortuitous characteristics it displays in itself. An individual of any family that possesses objectionable genetic material will pass it on to the next generation even though he or she does not mirror such unwanted traits in itself. It is far better to use an average animal from top stock than a top individual from average or below average stock as a breeding partner.

Often a great show dog produces average progeny while his little known brother, obscured by the shadow of the great winning dog's eminence, produces many above-average young, and generally from a poorer grade of bitches than attend the court of his illustrious brother. This is not so strange when we consider the fact that the individual animal is the custodian of his germ plasm and it is this inheritable material that produces, not the dog. In the case of the famous champion (with apologies to Perry Mason), due to variation in the germ plasm, the famous dog does not possess the happy combination of genetic attributes that his average brother does and so cannot produce stock of comparative value. Let me make it clear that when I write of "top" animals in reference to breeding I mean dogs within the breed that are great producers, not necessarily champions of the show ring for, as the example above points out, the two are not analogous.

Any of the various categories of breeding practice which I will outline can be followed for the betterment of your breed if used intelligently. Regardless of what practice one follows or prefers, there generally comes a time when it is necessary to incorporate one or more of the other forms or techniques into the breeding program in order to concentrate certain genetic traits, or to introduce new ones which are imperative for over-all balance.

Outcross breeding is not recommended as a constant practice even though it can be used to produce good stock. With this manner of production the breeder does not have control of the genetic material that fashions the living canine clay. There are times, I must admit, when some congenital defect or disease is found to have been transmitted by genetic material that is carried by one of the backbone strains of the breed, when outcross breeding can be the only answer to the problem. Rather, under ordinary circumstances, should this type of breeding be utilized as a valuable adjunct to other methods, a corrective measure that can bring new genetic values quickly to the

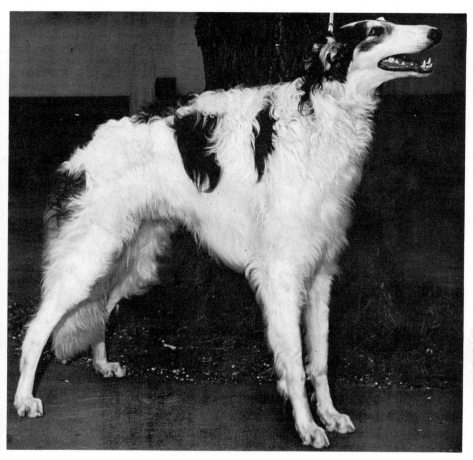

Many a top show dog produces only average progeny while a litter brother, failing a bit in conformation when compared to the celebrated winner and therefore not known and infrequently used at stud, can be genetically capable of producing much better-than-average stock.

Saint Bernard

Rottweiler

whelping pen. Truthfully, outcross breeding in any breed does not, as would be supposed by definition, cause the production of completely heterozygous young. The root stock of any breed is the same regardless of which breeding partners are used and, as we have previously shown, much of the stock which represents what we term outcrossing will show common ancestry within a few generations.

INBREEDING

By breeding father to daughter, half brother to half sister, son to mother and, the closest inbreeding of all, brother to sister, stability and purity of inherited material is obtained. Specifically, inbreeding concentrates both good features and faults, strengthening dominants and bringing recessives out into the open where they can be seen and evaluated. It supplies the breeder with the only close control he can have over prepotency and homozygosity, or the combining and

Breeds of similar structure and from the same or an adjacent area, are often interbred. The Cardigan and Pembroke Welsh Corgis are a prime example. This practice has been discontinued now and the two Corgi types are bred along distinct and separate lines.

balancing of similar genetic factors. Inbreeding does not produce degeneration, as so many people imagine. It merely concentrates weaknesses already present so that they come to the fore and can be recognized and eliminated. This applies to both physical and psychical hereditary transmission.

The most important phases of inbreeding are:

1. To choose as nearly faultless partners as is possible.

2. To cull, or select, rigidly from the resultant progeny.

3. To make particular note of the faults produced, especially if factors for crippling defects or congenital disease appear.

Selection is always important regardless of which breeding procedure is used, but in inbreeding it becomes imperative. Of particular interest is the fact that most successful inbreeding programs have used as a base one partner that was either inbred or linebred. The reason for this is that to the breeder the inbred animal represents a simplified breeding formula, a dog from whom certain results can almost always be depended upon in the breeding pen. Inbreeding, of course, brings out the faults as well as the virtues and defines them. Therefore the faults produced by inbreeding are the weaknesses in the line that must be eliminated, and for this reason are important.

There are many examples of extreme inbreeding over a period of generations in other animal and plant life. One of the most widely known were the experimental rats bred by Dr. Helen L. King, which were the result of over one hundred generations of direct brother to sister breeding. The result was bigger, finer rodents than the original breeding pair and entirely dependable uniformity. There are advertisements in certain journals published specifically for laboratories that offer rats, mice, and hamsters that are guaranteed to give uniform experimental results because the rodents offered for sale are the result of fifty or more generations of brother to sister inbreeding. Dr. Leon F. Whitney once bred and developed a beautiful strain of tropical fish, *Lebistes reticulatis*, commonly known as "Guppies", by consecutive brother to sister mating for from ten to fifteen generations. The author did the same for eight generations with a similar strain of *Lebistes reticulatis*. In both instances these decorative little fish began to decrease in size and color after approximately the third generation of inbreeding. There was a loss of vigor and breeding ability. Strict selection was adhered to. Then, from the fifth generation on, a change occurred for the better, and in each

Cardigan Welsh Corgi

Boxer

Originally the result of complete outcrossing between two contemporary breeds, the Sheng Trou, or Lhasa Apso, and the Chinese Pekingese, these three charming Shih Tzus represent a breed that possessed basic heterozigosity which had to be drastically lessened and controlled to hold breed type.

generation thereafter size, color, and vigor improved, and the end result was a tank of multi-colored water-jewels flashing flowing fins and tails of extravagant size and beauty, far bigger and better than the very fine original fish.

Genetic experiments with plants, vegetables, fish, birds, and living forms which we consider lower in the evolutionary scale than our beloved dogs, have shown that when two intensely inbred lines of consecutive brother to sister matings are crossed, the resultant progeny are larger than the original heterozygous stock and possess hybrid vigor such as the mongrel possesses, which enables him to exist even under environmental neglect. This type of breeding has been labelled *heterosis* and we will learn more about it toward the end of this chapter.

Can dog breeders indulge in such concentrated inbreeding as has been successfully attempted with other genetic material? We don't know, simply because, to our knowledge, it has never been tried. It would be an extremely expensive undertaking and would have to be approached on a coldly clinical level inviting no emotional envolvement with the dogs used. Experimental lines would first have to be selected that offer the least chance of hereditary weakness. Two

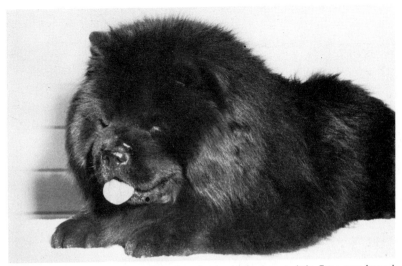

The black tongue of the Chow Chow is a fixed genetic characteristic. Type was formed by Chinese breeding masters when the breed was young, through close inbreeding. Weaknesses made apparent through drastic inbreeding can be controlled by one direct outcross.

or more lines of direct brother to sister inbreedings would have to be kept going, and in each breeding, culling and destroying would be necessary and the best pair kept as breeding partners for the next generation. It would also be necessary to keep at least one other line going as a form of insurance. Lethal faults, hitherto unsuspected in the stock, might become so drastically concentrated that the experiment could be brought to a premature conclusion, even if one had the time, money, and patience to attempt it. But such is the inherent character of germ plasm that one direct outcross would bring back complete normality to an inbred line drastically weakened by its own concentrated faults.

You will find that close inbreeding is necessarily at the roots of your breed as it is with every breed. In order to quickly establish the wanted type inbreeding had to be used to the dog or dogs that most closely approached the envisioned standard. Once the basic type was fixed by close inbreeding, selection for smaller virtues that would fit the breed ideal were consistently made with quick advantage taken of any mutation that furthered this concept. This is the way in which a breed is molded to a specific form.

It is essential that the breeder have a complete understanding of

Dachshund

Bullmastiff

the merits of inbreeding, for by employing this method skillfully results could be obtained to equal those found in other animal-breeding fields. It must be remembered that inbreeding in itself creates neither faults nor virtues, it merely strengthens and fixes them in the resulting progeny. If the basic stock used is generally good, possessing but few, and those minor, faults, then inbreeding will concentrate all those virtues which are so valuable in that basic stock. Inbreeding gives us great breeding worth by its unique ability to produce prepotency and unusual similarity of type. It exposes the "skeletons in the closet" by bringing to light hitherto hidden faults, so that they may be recognized and selected against. We do not correct faults by inbreeding therefore, we merely make them recognizable so they can be eliminated. The end result of inbreeding, coupled with rigid selection, is complete stability of the breeding material.

With certain strains inbreeding can be capricious, revealing organic weakness never suspected that result in decreased vitality, abnormalities (physical and mental), or lethal or crippling factors. Unfortunately it is not possible to foretell results when embarking upon such a program, even if seemingly robust and healthy breeding partners are used as a base. The best chance of success generally comes with the employment of dogs which themselves have been strongly inbred and have not been appreciably weakened by it in any way. This is proof that the stock has the ability to produce strength even under the most adverse conditions, and that it is inherently good, sound stock.

An interesting development frequently found in inbreeding is in the extremes produced. The average progeny from inbreeding is equal to the average from line-breeding, outcross breeding, etc., but the extremes are greater in scope than those produced by any of the other generally used methods of breeding. Inbreeding then, since it is capable of gathering together, concentrating, and presenting all the faults and all the virtues prevalent in each individual (genetically), is at once capable of producing the *best* and the *worst*, and these degrees can be found present in the same litter.

Here again, in inbreeding, we must avoid thinking in terms of human equations. Whether for good or ill, our dogs are man-made, and their destiny is in our hands. By selection we improve our animals, culling and killing misfits and monsters. Mankind indulges in no such purification of the race. He mates without any great mental calculation or plan for the future generation. His choice of a mate is both geographically and socially limited in scope. No one plans his matings for the "future benefit of the breed". Instead, he is blindly led by an emotion labelled "love", and sometimes by lesser romantics, "desire". Perish the thought that we should cast mud upon the limpid, scented waters of romance, but for our dogs we want something vastly better than the hit-and-miss *modus operandi* that has been the racial procedure of man.

BACKCROSSING

Another type of inbreeding, which is not practiced as much as it should be, is "backcrossing". Here we think largely in terms of the male dog, since the element of time is involved. The process involves finding a superior breeding male who is so magnificent in type (or who produces such magnificent type), that we wish to perpetuate his qualities and produce, as closely as we can, the prototype of this individual, or infuse our whole breeding line with his virtues. This excellent male is bred to a fine bitch capable of correcting any small faults the male might have genetically. The best female puppy is saved from the litter and, at the proper time, bred back to her sire, the exceptional male. Again, from this breeding, the best bitch whelp is saved and bred back to the male. This is continued as long as the selected male is capable of producing, or until weaknesses become apparent (if they do) that make it impractical to continue. If this excellent male seems to have acquired his superiority through the genetic influence of his mother, then the first breeding made should be son to mother, and the subsequent breedings as described above. If his sire seems to have contributed most to his excellence, then the best sister of his sire should be used for the first breeding.

The secret to success in backcrossing is to select, from each litter, the bitch that *most closely resembles the sire* for the next breeding. In this way the wanted type is perpetuated, generation after generation.

LINE-BREEDING

Line-breeding is a broader, less intense, employment of inbreeding that preserves valuable genetic characteristics by concentration and, in a more general sense, gives the breeder some control over specific

Cavalier King Charles Spaniel

Kerry Blue Terrier

Clumber Spaniel

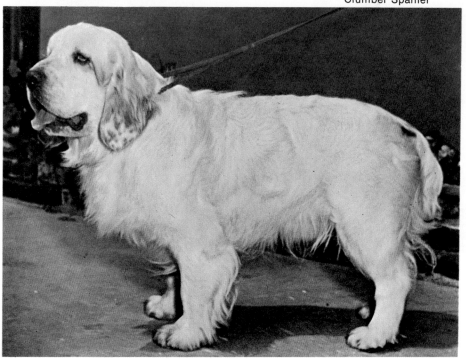

Through the clever application of the line-breeding
technique, a strain can be formed that will exhibit
similarity in its members and breed true. This breeding method allows an individual to evolve a
family that will influence type in the breed for
generations. These Shetland Sheepdogs illustrate
the closeness of conformation possible through
linebreeding.

traits. Through the agency of line-breeding "strains", or "families", can be originated within a breed which can be easily recognized by their similarity in type. Such breeding is not extreme and therefore relatively safe. It is also the method the neophyte is generally advised to employ for the very same reason (because it is safe) mentioned above.

Specifically, line-breeding entails the selection of breeding partners who have, in their genetic background, one or more common ancestors. These individuals (or individual) occur repeatedly within the first four or five generations, so that it can be assumed that their genetic influence molds the type of succeeding generations. It is an established fact that in most breeds success has crowned the efforts of breeders who, with knowledge and ability, have used line-breeding to build a strain carrying the kennel name.

The method varies in intensity so that some dogs may be strongly line-bred, while others are only remotely so. Selection is an important factor here, too, for if we line-breed to procure the specific type of certain fine animals (or one great individual), then we must select, in the succeeding generations, breeding stock which is the prototype of these dogs or that individual, or our reason for line-breeding is lost.

One of the chief dangers of line-breeding can be contributed personally by the breeder, the creator of the strain. Too often the breeder reaches a point where he selects breeding partners on pedigree alone, instead of by complete study and combining of pedigree, data, and individual partners to the breeding.

In some instances intense line-breeding, particularly when the individual (or individuals) used exhibit extreme prepotency, can have all the genetic power of direct inbreeding. The same name appearing as the grandfather on both the sire and dam lines stops the male lines of descent and if the animal is truly prepotent, he will definitely give freely of his genetic virtues to the grandchildren.

Not quite as heavily line-bred is the dog whose grandparents (let us say the two male grandparents) were litter brothers. Still more remote line-breeding would repeat the name of a particular dog, perhaps coupled with a litter brother or sister, three or four times in the fourth and fifth generation.

In any kind of close breeding, inbreeding or line-breeding, the same name must appear on both the sire and dam's pedigree. No matter how saturated one parent may be with a specific individual's heritage, it is not considered "in" or "line" breeding unless both upper and lower brackets of the pedigree share that name. In analyzing a pedigree for such data we designate the generation in which the common ancestor occurs, indicating the dividing line between the sire and dam lines with a dash. For example: if the name of a common ancestor upon which a particular dog has been line-bred appears once in the third generation and once in the fourth generation on the sire's side, and then is found once in the second generation and twice in the fourth generation on the dam's side, we indicate these line-breeding findings in the following manner: 3, 4 — 2, 4, 4 and attach the name of the individual designated to the pedigree generation numbers.

Of the many breeds in this country that have their roots in foreign soil, line-breeding is often indulged in by using prominent imported sires on line-bred bitches, then crossing the results so that the bitches on both sides of the pedigree show like line-breeding while the males, the sires of both the dog and bitch to be mated, are the imported studs.

The founding of a strain through line-breeding will be discussed more fully in Chapter 8. As an end result line-breeding gives the breeder enough control over the genetic material of the breed with which he is working that he is able to reproduce repeatedly, and over many generations, a certain type of animal bearing his personalized stamp in conformation.

OUTCROSS BREEDING

With this breeding technique partners are chosen whose pedigrees, within the first five or six generations, are free from common ancestry. As I have mentioned before, one cannot outcross in the true scientific sense of the term, since the genetic basis of all canines as individual breeds is based upon the germ plasm of a few selected animals from which the breed was formulated. To outcross completely, using the term literally (complete heterozygosity), it would be necessary to use an individual of an alien breed as one of the breeding partners.

For the breeder to exercise any control over the progeny of an outcross mating, one of the partners should be inbred or closely line-bred. The other partner should show, in itself and by the progeny test when bred to other partners, that it is dominant in the needed compensations that are one of the reasons for the outcross. Thus, by outcross breeding we bring new and needed characteristics into a strain, along with greater vigor and, generally, a lack of uniformity in the young. Greater uniformity can be achieved if the outcross is made between animals of similar family type.

Outcrossing has produced many excellent animals in all breeds, since this mode of breeding tends to conceal recessives and promote individual merit, while bringing greater vigor, strength and health to the dogs that are the result of such breeding. But since the outcross bred dog is heterozygous it is difficult to find his breeding formula. Outcrossed animals generally indicate lower breeding worth because favorable genetic combinations have been dispersed; inheritable groupings that could have given the breeder some kind of uniformity.

Outcross breeding can be likened to modifications made in a jigsaw puzzle. We have a puzzle composed of pieces of various shapes and sizes which, when fitted together, form a certain pattern. This

A stud can be prepotent even though he is the result of outcross breeding. This would seem to be in direct opposition to genetic theory, but objective investigation leads to the knowledge that close inbreeding is at the base of any breed so that no dog of a specific breed, is completely heterozygous.

puzzle is comparable to an inbred or line-bred strain. But in this puzzle there are a few pieces we would like to change, and in so doing change the finished puzzle pattern for the better. We outcross by removing some of the pieces and reshaping them to our fancy, remembering that these new shapes we introduce will affect the shapes of the adjoining pieces. These, the adjoining pieces, must then also be altered slightly for a perfect fit. When this has been successfully accomplished the finished pattern has been given new color and verve.

It sometimes happens that a line-bred or inbred bitch is outcross-bred to a stud possessed of an open pedigree. It would be assumed by the breeder that the bitch's family type would dominate in the resulting progeny, but this does not always happen. Occasionally such a stud proves to be strongly prepotent, and the young reflect his genetic qualities, not the dam's. Usually, in the next generation the genetic qualities of the dam become manifest.

Outcross breeding is generally used in what is called corrective, or compensation breeding, and to bring new genetic qualities to a line. When speaking of compensative or corrective breeding, I do not mean the breeding of extremes to achieve an intermediate effect. For example, you should not breed a barrel-ribbed dog to a very narrow-ribbed animal to arrive at the desired intermediate ribbing. The result of such breeding will generally be animals displaying both extremes, but none with the wanted ribbing (this is particularly true where both animals come from strains that have always exhibited these faults). Corrective, or compensation, breeding means the breeding of one partner, which is lacking or faulty in any specific respect, to an animal that is normal or excellent in the particular area in which the other partner is found wanting. In the resulting litter we can expect to find some young which display the desired improvement, especially if the wanted improvement is a known virtue of the strain from which the dog, used to compensate for the particular fault, has come.

One of the distinct virtues to be found in outcross breeding is its ability to bring, in one generation, strength and vigor back to a strain weakened by the faults inherent in its close breeding. It can also act as a decided check on the incidence of congenital diseases or ills that are concentrated and perpetuated by close breeding.

BACK-MASSING

Sometimes in a three, or even four, generation pedigree, we will see no evidence (or very little) of any close breeding but, if we extend the pedigree further we find what I have termed *"Back-massing"*, or a massing of the name of one stud. Usually the first two or three generations are the most important in any pedigree. But when you find a piling up of the genetic values of one individual in the background of a pedigree, even though several generations removed, the influence of that individual will be felt.

In one breed the author has seen such influence cause the appearance of a specific congenital disease which could only be held in abatement by constant outcrossing to animals who did not have any of that particular stud's breeding behind them. Back-massing can bring virtues as well as ills, but I have used this example to dramatize the influence back-massing can have within a breed.

HETEROSIS

This is a comparatively new field in genetic research. The results obtained in other fields (agricultural, and with swine and chickens) by the use of this method of breeding have been phenomenal. Extensive research is still continuing and, since genetic material can vary in its reaction and result to any given and unexplored breeding method, untried as yet with dogs (and perhaps never to be tried), this type of breeding should perhaps be not included here. But I think it will, in all probability, arouse as much interest in the reader as it has in the author.

Briefly and simply the basis of heterosis is the breeding together of selected brothers and sisters, and this is continued for many generations to establish strains that are completely homozygous (all gene pairs alike). It seems doubtful, to the writer, that absolute homozygosity can be attained, regardless of the number of generations of inbreeding, due to genetic variation and mutational effects. Yet here it is necessary to inbreed for enough generations to arrive at the most heterozygous result obtainable.

After three or four generations have been bred, test-cross matings are tried by crossing the several lines established by heterosis to determine which of the strain crossings will give the greatest improvements. The most usable strains are then maintained and the inbreeding within the original lines is continued.

The author indulged in this method of breeding using Budgerigars (Parakeets) as genetic material. The results paralleled those found in similar experiments with other genetic material. After the fifth generation the inbred lines displayed degeneration. Some improvement was shown by the eighth generation. Meanwhile several of my lines had lost their ability to either reproduce or adequately care for their young. In some instances lethal factors allowed no survival of chicks. Then, when I crossed the best two lines the results were dramatic. The progeny were very large, strong, vigorous, brilliantly plumaged birds, better and bigger by far than the starting stock.

The following emperic notes were made by me during the process of the experiment. A hypothesis, if you will, of this type of breeding with this specific avian material.

Could we, the breeders of this or any other country, use heterosis in the breeding of fine dogs such as this Lakeland Terrier? The question has no answer because this breeding method has never been tried with the canine species.

Notes on heterosis:

Heterosis $F_{1\ 2\ 3\ 4}$ etc. can be successfully crossed back into the best of the original (foundation) inbred stock that initially produced them.

Selection is of primary importance.

Select for: 1. Fertility (and early fertility).
           2. Major type virtues.

Heterozygous advantage ($K>1$) should be greater for those traits which exhibit strong inbreeding depression.

The use of partially inbred strains, selected for specific performance (fertility, hatchability, prolificacy, crop milk richness, etc.) will bring more rapid fixing of homozygous virtues in the inbred strains.

It is possible that heterosis will produce a greater number of mutations than occur in normal breeding practice.

Heterosis, it would seem, is accompanied by intermediate gene frequency equilibrium . . . or an essential and basic balance of chromatic design.

I suppose that you as a breeder realize, just as I have, that to some people, even novices in our own breeds, our deep absorption in the many aspects of breed betterment may seem silly or ridiculous. But wanton breeding practices have, in the past, almost destroyed fine breeds, and the genetic repercussion of breeding stupidity can echo down through generations, making mockery of our own intense, sometimes heartbreaking, and often humble, striving toward the ideal.

The brood bitch is the foundation of any kennel and the breeder's hope for the future. She is the living vehicle through which advancement toward a given ideal can be achieved by canny selection of a mate, and by the proper use of her precious genetic characteristics.

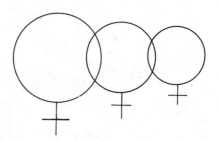

CHAPTER 6

THE BROOD BITCH

To the breeder a fine brood bitch is the center of all endeavor. Here is the mother within whom the seed will grow and be nourished. Here is the hope for advancement in the future. Truly if we want to succeed in bringing improvement to any breed, we must begin with the female, and she must be the best that we can possibly find. The productive value of the bitch is comparatively limited by seasonal vagary and this, in turn, increases the importance of every litter that she produces.

To begin breeding we must, of necessity, begin with a bitch as the foundation. The foundation of all things must be strong and as free from faults as possible or the structure we build upon it will crumble. The bitch we choose for our foundation female must then be a good bitch, superb in both structure mentality and character. She is the product of her germ plasm, and temperament, a most important facet of her being, must be analyzed so that we can compensate, in breeding, for any hidden mental faults that may lurk in her heritage. Structurally the good brood bitch should be strongly made and up to standard size. She should be deep in body, with a good spring of ribs and with ample room through the pelvic region. Weakness and delicacy are not the essence of femininity in dogs and should particularly be avoided in the brood bitch. I do *not* mean that a bitch should be coarse. She should be feminine, but strong and healthy.

A bitch comes in season first between the ages of six months and a year, according to the breed. Females of the smaller breeds come in season earlier than the larger breeds. Though this is an indication that nature considers her old enough and developed enough to breed, it is best to allow her to pass this first heat and plan to breed her when she next comes in season. This second period of ovulation should come within six months if her environment does not change. Daylight, which influences certain glands, seems to affect the ratio

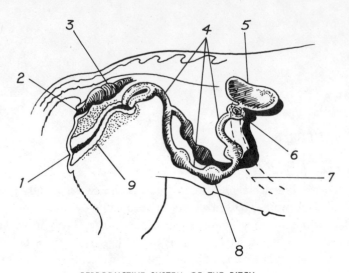

REPRODUCTIVE SYSTEM OF THE BITCH
1. Vulva 2. Anus 3. Rectum 4. Uterus 5. Kidney 6. Ovary 7. Ribs (indicated)
8. Developing embryo 9. Vagina

of time between heats, as does a complete change of environment.

Scientific studies of the incidence of seasonal variation in the mating cycles of bitches indicate that more bitches come in heat and are bred during the months of February and May than at any other time of the year. The figures used to make this study may not be completely reliable, since they were assembled through birth registrations in the American Kennel Club, and many breeders refrain from fall and winter matings so that they will not have winter or early spring litters when the ground is snowy, wet, or muddy.

If you are a breeder of any of the Toy breeds, it is best to depend on the stud dog you use to give you smaller size than on the brood bitch. If you do use a very small bitch and breed her to an equally tiny stud, either or both of the breeding partners may carry genetic determiners for larger size and the puppies may be so large that the bitch will have difficulty in whelping. On the other hand a small bitch who is well made with good spring of rib, good depth and a wide pelvis, might find it easier to whelp her litter than a larger bitch who does not have these structural virtues.

In the larger breeds it is often recommended that a bitch should be brought to her third season before breeding. There is no real proof that it is necessary to wait this long. In fact, should you breed your bitch at her second season, it will probably aid in giving her body more depth, better spring of rib, a greater maturity and grace.

When your bitch is approaching her period of heat and you intend to breed her, have her stool checked for intestinal parasites and, if there are any present, worm her. This is important, for worm larvae in the bloodstream of the bitch cross the placenta to infect the unborn pups, or the newly born whelps contract the eggs of these parasites at the mother's breast or from the surrounding environment. The result can be unthrifty pups that will never attain to the full flower of their genetic heritage.

Feed your bitch well as she approaches the time of mating. A good, well-balanced diet, such as she has been getting, is fine. Her appetite will increase during the preparatory stages of the mating cycle as her vulva begins to swell. But be careful that you do not accede to her greater demands at the feeding dish or she will become too fat. She will become restless, will urinate more frequently, and will allow male dogs to approach her, flirt with them, but not allow

Toy dogs reach breeding maturity earlier than the larger breeds. To avoid trouble in whelping, the Toy bitch should be up to size and well made. The stud used can be very tiny to get the wanted smallness. Some Toys, such as these Pugs, are not easy whelpers.

copulation. Within the bitch other changes are taking place at this stage. Congestion has begun in the reproductive tract, and the horns of the uterus and the walls of the vagina have begun to thicken.

The first signs of blood from the vulva ushers in the second stage of the mating cycle. In some bitches there is so little blood that it is not noticed by the owner. Frequently the bitch will keep herself clean with the same results. This means that the breeder does not know definitely when the first sign of red made its appearance and so cannot be certain of the exact dates in the cycle. Other bitches bleed throughout the cycle. Due to all these circumstances the breeder must depend on other signs to tell him when the proper day has come to breed the bitch. During this second stage the bitch becomes even more playful with other dogs but still will not allow copulation. Congestion within the bitch reaches a high point during this period. Ova develop within the follicles of the ovaries and, normally, the red discharge gradually loses its richness of color and turns eventually to pink, which color in turn becomes lighter and lighter until the fluid becomes straw colored and is no longer obvious.

The bitch's vulva is more swollen, and she is increasingly more playful and flirtatious with dogs of the opposite sex, a condition very trying to the males with whom she comes in contact since she will still not permit them to breed to her. This period is generally of

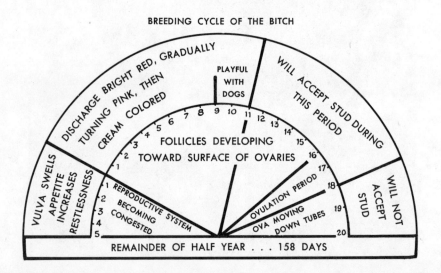

BREEDING CYCLE OF THE BITCH

about ten days duration, but the time varies with the individual bitch. Rather than rely upon any set time period, it is best to conclude that this part of the period will end when the bitch will stand for the stud and permit copulation. This generally occurs at about the tenth day, but can take place as early as the fourth or fifth day of this period, and the author has known of bitches who will not permit copulation until as late as the seventeenth day of this second period.

The third period of the cycle is, then, the acceptance period. The bitch swings her hind end toward the dog, her tail will arch up and she will invite copulation. Sometimes the stud may have to tease her for a time but she will eventually give in. If she doesn't, then she must be muzzled and held for the dog to mount. The bitch may be sensitive and yelp and pull frantically away as though in pain when the stud's penis touches the lining of the vagina. If this occurs several times, it is best to wait another day until the sensitivity leaves this region. But do not wait too long, for maiden bitches often act this way, and if you allow too much time to go by in consideration of her touchiness, you might miss making the breeding entirely.

A very definite indication that the bitch is in the acceptance period is the softness, large size and flaccidity of the vulva, from which all congestion and firmness has gone. Within the bitch the ovarian follicles have been growing ever bigger and, approximately midway in the acceptance period, some of them burst and the eggs are ready for fertilization. If the female has had a normal mating cycle, which is to be hoped for, the best time to breed her is about the thirteenth to fourteenth day of the mating cycle, when ovulation takes place. This time also varies with the individual bitch, so that until you have bred her once or twice and feel that you know the best time to breed her to insure success, it is best to do so on the eleventh day and every other day thereafter until her period of acceptance is over.

It is generally only possible to indulge in the number of breedings mentioned above if the stud dog is in your possession or is owned by a nearby friend. One good breeding that results in a fast tie of from 5 minutes to 30 minutes duration is actually all that is necessary to make the bitch pregnant, provided that breeding is made at the right time. If copulation is forced before the bitch is ready, the result is no puppies at all or a small litter, since the sperm must wait for ovulation inside the bitch and the life of the sperm is limited, particularly when exposed to the body heat of the female. The acceptance period ceases rather abruptly and is signalled by a definite resistance of the bitch to the male's advances.

Bitches shipped long distances to specific studs for breeding too often do not produce litters. There are many reasons for this but chief among them is the fact that the bitch was probably not bred to the stud at the right time due to time wasted in transit, or because the stud, being popular, was only put to her once, and then at the wrong time. But, if your bitch fails to conceive from a good and proper breeding, do not immediately put the blame on the stud dog. In most cases it is the fault of the bitch or, more realistically, the owner of the bitch for not adequately timing the mating. No matter how fertile a stud dog may be, the sperm he ejects must have a target, the eggs the bitch produces and, if they are not there the result will be no pregnancy.

There is one way which the author has found to be constantly sure, because it will remove most of the guesswork from breeding. Have your veterinarian make a vaginal smear and examine it under his microscope. He will be able to tell approximately what stage of the cycle the bitch is in and when ovulation will occur. Your veterinarian can also help you if you happen to have a bitch who produces only a very small number of puppies, or less than one third of the number one would expect from her particular breed. The veterinarian can utilize drugs, by injection, that will stimulate the necessary hormones to produce many more ova and also trigger the release of the ova. These fertility drugs (labelled FSH and HCG, with a possibility of more on the market and bearing trade names by the time this book is published) have proved to be extremely successful.

If your bitch is a maiden it is best to breed her the first time to an older stud who knows his business and is an easy breeder. When you bring her to the stud, and if there are adjoining wire-enclosed runs, put the stud in one run and the bitch in an adjacent one. They will make overtures through the wire and later, when the stud is brought to the bitch, copulation generally occurs quickly. It is always best to place the bitch manually in the proper position to be bred and hold her there during the tie so she will not attempt to break away or sit down.

Normal physiology of the reproductive system can be interrupted or delayed by disturbance, disease, or illness in any part of the bitch's body. A sick bitch will therefore not come in season, though

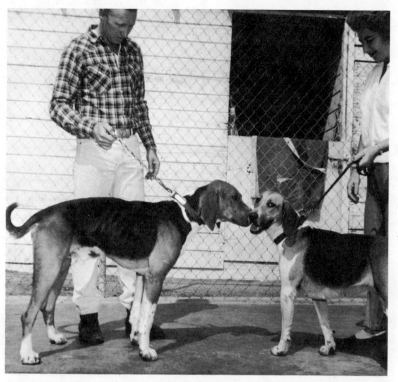

Introduce the male to the female and allow them a short time to become acquainted. This interval generally makes the subsequent mating go smoother and aids in calming excited or frightened bitches.

it is her time to do so, until after she has completely recovered from her ailment and has returned to normal. Bitches past their prime and older tend to have a shorter mating cycle and so must be bred sooner than young bitches to assure pregnancy. There are always the exceptions to the rule, however. The author owns an imported bitch at this time who is six years old and must be bred at from the eighteenth to the twentieth day in the cycle to assure pregnancy. When she is bred on the eighteenth day she will whelp 65 days afterward.

During copulation and the resulting and wanted tie, you should assist the stud dog owner as much as possible. If the stud evinces pain when he attempts to force his penis into the vulva, check the bitch. In virgin bitches you may find a web of flesh which runs vertically across the vaginal opening and causes pain to the dog when his penis is pushed against it. This web must be broken by hooking your finger around it and pulling until it rips, after which the breeding can be consummated. During the tense and frenetic excitement of the breeding and while the tie is in effect, speak to the bitch quietly and keep her from moving until the tie is broken, then snap on a leash and remove her from the presence of the stud and allow her to indulge in a period of retrospective quiet.

Do not allow any other male dogs to come near her until you are absolutely positive that the mating cycle is over and her time of acceptance has definitely gone by. She can (and many bitches have) become impregnated by a second dog and whelp a litter of mixed paternity, some of the puppies sired by the first dog and others fathered by the second dog to breed her. Sometimes a bitch is bred to a selected stud dog just before she ovulates. The sperm of this dog will remain alive and fertile within the bitch's body until the eggs break down the next day. But the next day the bitch, somehow or other, gets out of her pen (or wherever she is being kept) and another male breeds to the bitch, the sperm of the two dogs that have bred to her mix within her and both become the sires of the resulting litter. It is an exceedingly strange fact that, though it is often difficult to make the breeding you desire (and have paid a fat stud fee to consummate), it takes little more time than the beginning of a scream for any other undesirable male to breed to your bitch and be charmingly tied for an hour or more. It is the little, humorous incidents of this type that cause even the most relaxed of fanciers to develop ulcers.

Let us assume that your bitch was in good health and you have had a good breeding to the stud of your choice at the proper time in the bitch's mating cycle to insure pregnancy. The male sperm has fertilized the eggs and life begins. The pups will be whelped in from fifty-nine to sixty-three days after the day of the breeding. Every bit of food you give the bitch from now until the time of birth will be aiding in the fetal development of the whelps within her. Be sure she is being provided with enough milk to produce calcium for bone-building; meat for phosphorus and iron; fat, cereal, and all the essential vitamins and minerals. A vitamin and mineral supplement should be incorporated in her diet but used moderately. If she is being fed a good commercial dog food as a base it will be

Perpetual Whelping Chart

	1	2	3	4	5	6	7	8	9	10	11	12	13	14	15	16	17	18	19	20	21	22	23	24	25	26	27	28	29	30	31
Bred—Jan.	1	2	3	4	5	6	7	8	9	10	11	12	13	14	15	16	17	18	19	20	21	22	23	24	25	26	27	28	29	30	31
Due—March (→April)	5	6	7	8	9	10	11	12	13	14	15	16	17	18	19	20	21	22	23	24	25	26	27	28	29	30	31	1	2	3	4
Bred—Feb.	1	2	3	4	5	6	7	8	9	10	11	12	13	14	15	16	17	18	19	20	21	22	23	24	25	26	27	28			
Due—April (→May)	5	6	7	8	9	10	11	12	13	14	15	16	17	18	19	20	21	22	23	24	25	26	27	28	29	30	1	2			
Bred—Mar.	1	2	3	4	5	6	7	8	9	10	11	12	13	14	15	16	17	18	19	20	21	22	23	24	25	26	27	28	29	30	31
Due—May (→June)	3	4	5	6	7	8	9	10	11	12	13	14	15	16	17	18	19	20	21	22	23	24	25	26	27	28	29	30	31	1	2
Bred—Apr.	1	2	3	4	5	6	7	8	9	10	11	12	13	14	15	16	17	18	19	20	21	22	23	24	25	26	27	28	29	30	
Due—June (→July)	3	4	5	6	7	8	9	10	11	12	13	14	15	16	17	18	19	20	21	22	23	24	25	26	27	28	29	30	1	2	
Bred—May	1	2	3	4	5	6	7	8	9	10	11	12	13	14	15	16	17	18	19	20	21	22	23	24	25	26	27	28	29	30	31
Due—July (→August)	3	4	5	6	7	8	9	10	11	12	13	14	15	16	17	18	19	20	21	22	23	24	25	26	27	28	29	30	31	1	2
Bred—June	1	2	3	4	5	6	7	8	9	10	11	12	13	14	15	16	17	18	19	20	21	22	23	24	25	26	27	28	29	30	
Due—August (→Sept.)	3	4	5	6	7	8	9	10	11	12	13	14	15	16	17	18	19	20	21	22	23	24	25	26	27	28	29	30	31	1	
Bred—July	1	2	3	4	5	6	7	8	9	10	11	12	13	14	15	16	17	18	19	20	21	22	23	24	25	26	27	28	29	30	31
Due—September (→Oct.)	2	3	4	5	6	7	8	9	10	11	12	13	14	15	16	17	18	19	20	21	22	23	24	25	26	27	28	29	30	1	2
Bred—Aug.	1	2	3	4	5	6	7	8	9	10	11	12	13	14	15	16	17	18	19	20	21	22	23	24	25	26	27	28	29	30	31
Due—October (→Nov.)	3	4	5	6	7	8	9	10	11	12	13	14	15	16	17	18	19	20	21	22	23	24	25	26	27	28	29	30	31	1	2
Bred—Sept.	1	2	3	4	5	6	7	8	9	10	11	12	13	14	15	16	17	18	19	20	21	22	23	24	25	26	27	28	29	30	
Due—November (→Dec.)	3	4	5	6	7	8	9	10	11	12	13	14	15	16	17	18	19	20	21	22	23	24	25	26	27	28	29	30	1	2	
Bred—Oct.	1	2	3	4	5	6	7	8	9	10	11	12	13	14	15	16	17	18	19	20	21	22	23	24	25	26	27	28	29	30	31
Due—December (→Jan.)	3	4	5	6	7	8	9	10	11	12	13	14	15	16	17	18	19	20	21	22	23	24	25	26	27	28	29	30	31	1	2
Bred—Nov.	1	2	3	4	5	6	7	8	9	10	11	12	13	14	15	16	17	18	19	20	21	22	23	24	25	26	27	28	29	30	
Due—January (→Feb.)	3	4	5	6	7	8	9	10	11	12	13	14	15	16	17	18	19	20	21	22	23	24	25	26	27	28	29	30	31	1	
Bred—Dec.	1	2	3	4	5	6	7	8	9	10	11	12	13	14	15	16	17	18	19	20	21	22	23	24	25	26	27	28	29	30	31
Due—February (→March)	2	3	4	5	6	7	8	9	10	11	12	13	14	15	16	17	18	19	20	21	22	23	24	25	26	27	28	1	2	3	4

145

adequately supplied with most of the necessary food elements. She must be fed well for her own maintenance and for the development of the young "in utero", particularly during the last 30 days of gestation. She should not, however, be given an excess of food. The pregnant bitch must never be allowed to become obese for it will hamper her greatly in whelping.

During this time she will begin to show the fact of her pregnancy. She will take on a look of sleek beauty, her coat will shine as it never has before. At about the thirtieth to the thirty-fifth day after breeding it is possible to determine pregnancy by palpation. It generally takes an expert, one who has had long experience in palpating, to actually feel with his fingers the tiny lumps that are the embryos forming in the bitch. If you wish to be sure that the breeding has been successful your veterinarian can take an X ray of the reproductive tract of your bitch. If you will just be patient a few days more the swelling of the female's abdomen will be hint enough that she is pregnant.

Your bitch, her run, her house and bed, should be free of worm and flea eggs. She should be allowed a moderate amount of free exercise in the prenatal period to keep her fit and muscularly healthy. If she had not had enough exercise prior to breeding and you wish to harden and reduce her, accustom her to the exercise gradually and it will do her a great deal of good. Allow her to have normal exercise but do not permit her to indulge in unaccustomed, abrupt, or violent exercise, or she might abort, though it is truly remarkable what most bitches can take during this period without losing their puppies.

The pups develop in the horns of the uterus, not the "tubes" (Fallopian tubes), as is commonly thought. As the puppies develop the horns of the uterus lengthen and the walls expand until the uterus may become as long as three and a half feet in dogs the size of Weimaraners, German Shepherds, Goldens, etc., if they are carrying a large litter.

A month before the bitch is due to whelp, incorporate fresh liver in her diet two or three times a week. This helps to keep her free of constipation and, aside from the actual value as a food, it will aid in the coming, necessary production of milk for the litter. If the litter is going to be a small one she will not show much outward sign until late in the gestation period. If the litter is going to be normal or large the bitch will begin to exhibit a distention of the abdomen at about thirty-five days after fertilization. Her appetite will have been increasing during this time and gradually the fact of her pregnancy will become more and more evident.

Several days before she is due to whelp, the whelping box should be prepared. It should be located in a dimly lit area removed from disturbance by other dogs or humans. Build the whelping box out of plywood and make it square with adequate room for the bitch and several puppies to inhabit without crowding. It should be enclosed on all sides and arranged so that extra boards can be applied to the sides to keep the pups from getting out, as they grow, after whelping and weaning. Put a small railing around the box a bit higher from the floor than the height of a few days old pup. This will prevent a

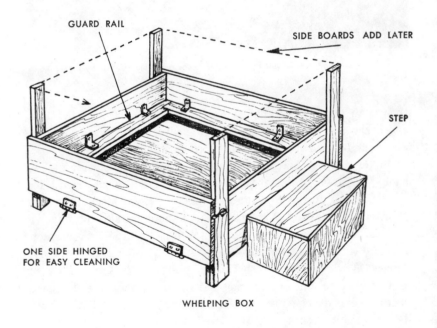

WHELPING BOX

careless bitch from crushing a puppy to death behind her. On the floor of the box lay a well fitted piece of rubber matting or oilcloth that can be removed and cleaned when necessary. Each breeder seems to have their own preference in the matter of bedding. I like oat straw or rye straw, because it can be hollowed out in the center to form a saucer shape and the whelps kept in the hollow part where

The whelping box of this Foxhound bitch has a rail made of metal pipes.

they can't crawl away. The bitch can curl right around her litter and everyone is cozy. During whelping several thicknesses of newspaper can be used at the bottom of the box and removed and disposed of as they become soiled from the whelping. A step outside the box should be provided to make it easier for the bitch to enter and leave.

The bitch, during this time, produces a great many hormones. Besides pituitary and ovarian hormones there are also hormones in the placenta and the urine, the ovarian follicles produce a hormone and the luteal bodies produce progesterone and relaxin, two hormones. A very important hormone, prolactin, is secreted by the pituitary at the time of whelping and it causes the milk to be manufactured and develops the maternal instinct in the bitch that makes her mother and care for her whelps. These hormones are chemical in composition, are secreted by the glands, act as body regulators and are moved throughout the body by blood and lymph, the circulating fluids. If your bitch has been bred to some undesirable male and you wish to prevent conception, take her to your veterinarian and he will use injections of extracts from some of these same hormones to prevent pregnancy or to cause the bitch to abort.

As the time approaches for whelping the bitch will become restless, she will refuse food and begin to make her nest. Her temperature will drop approximately one degree within about 24 hours of the time she will whelp, and she will exhibit a definite dropping down through the abdomen. Labor begins with pressure from within that forces the puppies toward the pelvis. The bitch generally twists around as the puppy is being expelled to lick the amniotic fluid that accompanies birth. Sometimes the sac surrounding the puppy will burst from pressure. If it doesn't the puppy will be born in the sac, a thin, membranous material called the fetal envelope. The navel cord (umbilical cord) runs from the puppy's navel to the afterbirth, or placenta. If the bitch is left alone at whelping time she will rip the fetal caul (and in the process shake up the puppy forcing air into its lungs), bite off the navel cord and eat the sac, cord and placenta. Should the cord be broken off during birth so that the placenta remains in the bitch, it will generally be expelled with the birth of the next whelp. Incidently, new experimentation seems to

This five weeks old litter of Retriever pups are in a vinyl lined box.

indicate that the longer (within reason) the umbilical cord is allowed to remain without being cut or bitten off, the less chance there is of respiratory ills. This cord should not be cut or bitten too close to the body of the pup. It will dry up and fall off in a very few days.

It is best for the breeder to be present when the bitch whelps. This is particularly true of young bitches having their first whelping, and of breeds that are notoriously difficult whelpers. Most breeders take on many of the tasks of whelping themselves and keep the placentas in a small box so that they can be counted against the number of puppies born to be certain that they have all been expelled by the time whelping is over. It is not necessary to tie up the end of the umbilical cord if you cut it, and it is not necessary to attempt to sterilize your hands or the implements you use while helping the bitch to whelp. The puppies will be practically surrounded with bacteria of all kinds from the moment they are born, some benign and others not benign which they are born equipped to combat.

If the bitch seems to be having difficulty expelling a particularly large pup you can help by wrapping a towel around your hands to

Even though your bitch may be of a breed that whelps without trouble, if she is young and having her first litter, it is best to aid her.

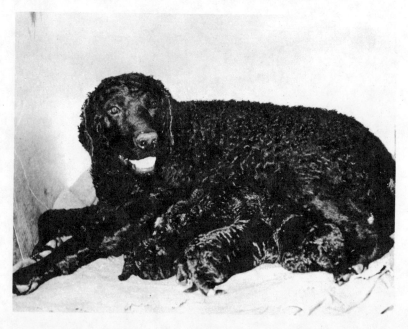

give you purchase, grasping the partly passed pup gently and, as the bitch presses to expel the pup, blend with her rhythm and gently pull. The puppies can be born head or tail first, either way is normal and common. As the pups are born, the sac broken and the cord snipped, dry them gently but vigorously with a towel and put them at the mother's breast, first squeezing some milk to the surface of the nipple, then opening their mouths for the entrance of the teat. You may have to hold them there by the head until they begin sucking.

After several puppies have been born in rapid succession an interval of time may elapse before another is born. If the bitch is a slow whelper and seems to be laboring hard after one or more pups have come, regular injections of Pitocin or Pituitrin (the former brings less nausea), at three hour intervals should be administered hypodermically into the hind leg. After the bitch has seemingly completed her whelping it is good practice to administer another shot of the same drug (intramuscularly) to make sure that no last puppy, alive or dead, is still unborn. Never use either of these drugs

A black and tan Hound bitch with her litter of fifteen puppies. The ability to produce large litters is governed by hereditary factors, assuming that the bitch is bred at the correct time.

unless she has whelped at least one puppy. As a matter of fact, it is probably better, unless you have had a good deal of experience in such matters, to call your veterinarian and let him administer any drugs that may be necessary.

Some time after the litter has been born offer the bitch some warm milk. Allow her to rest quietly and enjoy the new sensation of motherhood for several hours. Then insist she leave her litter to go out and relieve herself. Feed her well with additional feedings of milk twice a day. Don't be alarmed if she does not show any milk before the first puppy's birth. Sometimes it appears before and sometimes only when the pups begin to nurse, since it is manufactured by glands from blood while the whelps are at the udders.

There are several ills that may befall the bitch during gestation and whelping. Eclampsia, sometimes called milk fever, is perhaps most common. This is a metabolic disturbance brought on by a deficiency of calcium in the diet. Plenty of milk and good all around nutrition will aid in avoiding this condition. Symptoms of eclampsia are troubled shaking, wild expression, muscular rigidity and a high

Puppies grow rapidly and are a constant drain on the bitch. She should therefore be fed well and frequently to supply the whelps' avid demands and so that she herself will keep in good health and condition.

temperature. If she should exhibit these symptoms the condition can be quickly remedied by an injection of calcium gluconate in a vein. Should you have an old bitch who resorbs her fetuses and cannot carry them to full term, your veterinarian can help her with the aid of stilbestrol*

Mastitis, an udder infection, can cause the death of the puppies. It is often mistaken by the uninformed for "acid milk", a condition that seldom exists in dogs because a bitch's milk is naturally acid. Mastitis cuts off part of the milk supply and the whelps either die of starvation due to the lack of sufficient milk, or die of infection contracted from the infected milk. Your veterinarian should be consulted immediately if this occurs.

It is not necessary to massage the dam's breasts at weaning time, with or without camphorated oil. They will cake naturally and quit secreting milk if left completely alone. Growths, infections, injuries, cysts, and other and various ailments can affect the female reproductive system and must be taken care of by your veterinarian.

The great majority of bitches who have been well cared for and well fed are strong and healthy and the bearing of litters is a natural procedure, the normal function of the female of the species to bear and rear the next generation and, in so doing, fulfill her precious destiny.

---

* Author's note: There are new drugs for specific purposes constantly marketed by the drug manufacturers who service veterinarians. Your veterinarian can acquaint you with the newest and best.

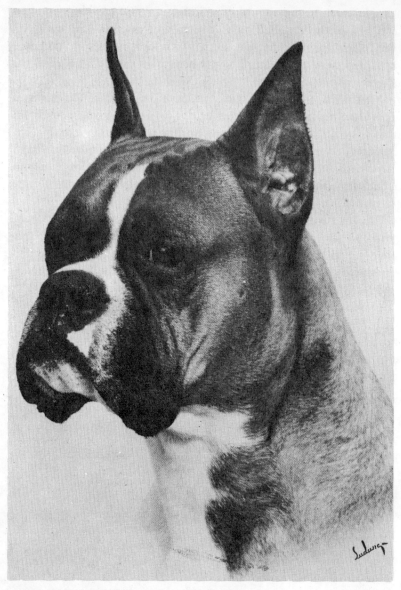

The inherited pattern of the popular stud dog can
fashion type over a large area, and his genetic
influence can be felt, for good or ill, for many
generations.

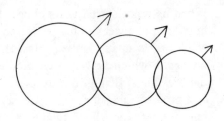

CHAPTER 7

THE STUD DOG

We have said that the importance of the bitch is unrivaled when we think of breeding, and this statement is true, for without the mother there would be no young, her womb is where all life begins. Why, then, do we pay so much attention to the male lines of descent? Why are the fine males considered so terribly important, so precious?

The reason is that stud dogs tend to mold the aspects of the breed on the whole and in any given country, or locality, to a much greater extent than do brood bitches. While the brood bitch is all-important to the individual breeder and can control type in a kennel, the stud dog can control type over a much larger area. This truth can be ascertained by the application of a simple mathematics.

Let us assume that the average litter is comprised of five puppies. The brood bitch will produce, then, a maximum of ten puppies a year if she is bred every season. In that same year a popular, good producing, well-publicized stud dog may be used on the average of three times weekly (many name studs, in various breeds, have been used even more frequently over a period of several years). This popular stud can therefore sire approximately fifteen puppies a week, employing the figures mentioned above, or seven hundred and eighty puppies a year. Compare this total to the bitch's yearly output of ten puppies and you will readily see why any one stud dog wields a much greater influence over the breed in general than does a specific brood bitch.

A well cared for stud dog will remain fertile generally for many more years than will a bitch. One dog that comes to mind immediately in this reference is the famous Cocker Spaniel stud, Red Brucie.

When he was thirteen years of age this great sire was bred to seven bitches in one week. This proved to be the last week of his life . . . which was probably only a coincidence! Incidently, all seven of the bitches to whom he was bred produced fine litters of puppies from the breedings. Being bred to seven bitches in one week was not, by any means, unusual for this Cocker stud. He became known as a fine sire early and lived a long and fruitful life, giving more to his breed than any other Cocker before or since his time. Red Brucie never became a champion in the show ring, but was certainly a champion in the stud paddock.

Red Brucie was but one of many great stud dogs in many breeds who were used extensively and over a period of many long years. I can call to mind a famous Poodle stud, Ch. Pulaski's Masterpiece, who was also well patronized by Toy Poodle bitch owners, and a great German Shepherd, Grimm von der Fahrmuhle, who was still siring large, fine litters at thirteen years of age. Pfeffer v. Bern, another Shepherd import was kept constantly busy as a stud, as was the famous imported Great Dane, Czardas v. Eppeleinsprung- Noris. I could go on indefinitely naming dogs in many breeds who were used extensively and over a long period of time at stud.

The above information also answers a question often asked by breeders, namely, "How often can a stud dog be used without harm to him, or without lowering his ability to produce large, healthy litters?" The answer is, as many times as he can be used without harm to him or without lowering his ability to produce large, healthy litters! This ability, like so many other aptitudes, is personal, varying with the individual. I would say, though, that any healthy stud dog should be able to breed three bitches a week without harm to himself . . . and certainly without harm to his owner when one considers the stud fees asked for good sires.

A famous German breeder wrote: "Modern breeding research has taught us that it is not so much the appearance of the animal that indicates its breeding values, but rather the hereditary picture, which means the sum total of the qualities and characteristics which it has inherited from its ancestors." This statement is as true today as when it was written in 1930! And is particularly applicable to the stud dog.

I have mentioned before, in some previous chapter, that many a great show champion would be greatly overshadowed in the breeding pen by a brother of little renown. The reason for this is that the above average dog will sire puppies that drop down to the "norm" because all extremes tend to breed toward the average (whether the extremes are good or bad). If this were not true, the great show champions would sire many more fine animals than they do with the opportunities they have of being bred to so many beautiful bitches so frequently. Check the number of excellent dogs sired by any top champion stud dog in any breed against the number of puppies he has sired within any given time period, and you will find that the number of top get are comparatively few. Often the brother of the top show dog is a better bet as a stud because he has approximately inherited the happy combination of genetic traits that produced the better known brother, and can pass them on, when properly used, to his offspring.

The care of the stud dog follows the same pattern as the care of any other dog; a balanced diet, clean quarters, plenty of exercise, and

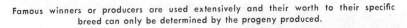

Famous winners or producers are used extensively and their worth to their specific breed can only be determined by the progeny produced.

a little affection. Though it is against most of the advice previously written or given on the subject, I recommend that the stud should be used for breeding for the first time when he is about twelve months old. Many small breed studs are used even before this age, but I am referring to dogs of breeds that are on the large side, that range in weight from seventy-five pounds up, and in height from twenty-two inches at the shoulder upward. The dog is as capable of siring a litter of fine and healthy pups at this age as he ever will be.

There are a few recommendations, however, that I wish to make if you do use your future stud dog this early in life. Breed him the first time to an older, steady, knowing bitch who has been bred several times before, is a very easy breeder and is entirely ready to accept him. Aid him if ncessary in this first sexual adventure but quietly and, if possible, so that he is not too much aware of your help. Allow nothing to disturb him during copulation. In fact the object

REPRODUCTIVE SYSTEM OF MALE

1. Prostate 2. Rectum 3. Anus 4. Section of pelvic bone 5. Testicle 6. Scrotum 7. Bulb (part of Penis) 8. Penis 9. Sheath 10. Vas deferens 11. Bladder

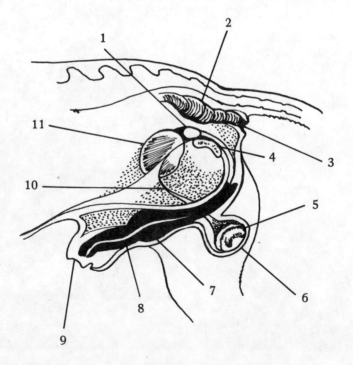

The stud dog must have both testicles, plainly visible and down in their sac (scrotum). If only one is present the dog is a monorchid. If both are missing the animal is a chryptorchid. Orchidism is a hereditary fault and an animal exhibiting this fault should not be used for breeding.

of this initial breeding is to see that all goes smoothly and easily. If you succeed in this aim, the young dog will become a willing and eager stud for the rest of his life, a circumstance devoutly to be wished for as there is nothing more exasperating than a reluctant stud dog. If all goes well with this initial breeding you will have a stud dog that is a pleasure to own and to use.

After this use him sparingly (and always on older, quiet, easily bred bitches), until he has reached sixteen to seventeen months of age. From that time on he can be used at least once or twice a week until he is two years old when he can be utilized for breeding as often as he is capable of being bred without showing wear.

The male organs vital for reproduction consist of: a pair each of testicles, where the sperm is produced; epididymis, in which the sperm are stored; and vas deferentia, through which the sperm are transported. The dog possesses no seminal vesicle as does man. But like man, the male dog is always in an active state of reproduction and can be used for breeding at any time.

The sperm are stored in the long, twisting tube, the epididymis; not with the semen, which is found in the prostate gland. When the stud mounts the bitch and successfully breeds to her so that an emission occurs, the semen is discharged from the prostate gland and, through suction and rhythmatic contraction (of the vas deferens), the sperm are drawn rapidly along the sperm tubes to mix with the semen. In just one emission the dog may discharge many million sperm. If you saw these tiny rods through a microscope you would realise why the sperm swarm must be so great, for many of the sperm are not normal and nature takes no chances, if she can help it, in the perpetuation of the race. Some of the sperm are two headed, some with too tiny a head, others have two stems, or crooked stems, but even with a multitude of crippled, useless sperm in each emission there are so many healthy ones that there are more than enough to hit any number of the eggs which are their targets.

There is a bone in the dog's penis and behind this bone is a group of very sensitive nerves which cause a violent thrusting-forward reflex when pressure is applied. The canine penis, unlike most other animals', has a bulbous enlargement at its base that can enlarge enormously under sexual stress.

The testicles are located outside the body in their own specific sacs, the scrotum. Sperm must be manufactured and stored at a much cooler temperature than that of the dog's body heat. The testicles develop originally inside the puppy's body and move downward through small openings in the abdominal wall and, at the time of birth, the testicles (if normal) are out of the puppy's body and immediately in front of the scrotum.

If the testicles (both of them) fail to descend at all, the dog is called a cryptorchid and the condition of being bereft of testicles, cryptorchidism. This signifies that the testicles have remained in the abdomen or have come through the abdominal rings but not descended enough to occupy the scrotum. Such dogs are inevitably sterile for, though they can perform the act of copulation and even eject spermatozoa (sperm), the heat of the body has rendered infertile any and all sperm that they discharge. Anorchidism is a parallel ill —a complete lack of testicles.

A monorchid is a male dog who exhibits but one testicle in its proper place, the other one having failed to descend into the scrotum. Monorchids can technically be used for breeding and will produce

This litter of Dingo puppies was born in the Berlin Zoo and sired by an eight months old male. The Dingo is the native Australian wild dog and, since it is the only placental mammal among the many marsupials found in Australia, it is thought to have migrated from the Asiatic mainland with the Aborigines of the "Down Under" continent.

puppies, but since orchidism in any form is a congenital and gene-linked fault and the worst kind of recognized physical unsoundness, dogs that are monorchids should never, but *never*, be bred to.

The terms used above are to designate animals with either one or no testicles provided the condition is not due to an accident or surgery. Cryptorchidism actually means "hidden testicle". Orchidism in either form, either partial or complete, is only a matter of degree genetically, and a monorchid, able to breed and produce young, can get full cryptorchidism as well as normals and monorchids in a litter. The worst part of this curse of orchidism is the fact that it is a

161

recessive and can be carried by the female of the species as well as the male. In the case of the female it is, of course, completely hidden and can be handed down from one generation to the next, *ad infinitum*, if carried by only the bitches. As a recessive it can also be carried in a hidden state by the males, but it will become obvious when the recessives meet and are pure for the trait. In bitches it behaves much like a sex-linked characteristic, and some researchers have declared it to be just that.

The growth downward of the testicles toward the scrotum is under the influence of an anterior pituitary gland hormone (manufactured synthetically now under the name A.P.L.). The testicles before birth, while in the abdomen, adhere to the peritoneum, which is the tissue that lines the abdomen. The peritoneum grows downward through the abdominal rings and into the scrotum carrying the testicles with it. The drug mentioned above (A.P.L.) or one of similar, new drugs, can sometimes stimulate the descent of the testicles in young puppies, if injected early enough, and make the pup normal. If both testicles have been removed from a dog that was normal it is called castration and the dog is a castrate *not* a cryptorchid.

Heat, as we have seen, kills sperm, but sperm can be stored outside of the dog's body if the container that holds it is kept refrigerated. I am sure you are aware of the fact that cows of many breeds can be brought to insemination stations run by the agricultural department, and there be artificially inseminated with the stored sperm of famous, tested bulls (great herd sires) that are long since dead. The A.K.C. frowns on such practice in dogs, but will accept registration on a litter that is the result of artificial insemination if the litter owner can produce sworn statements from the veterinarian who gathered the sperm from the stud, and the verterinarian who injected the sperm into the bitch (generally the same veterinarian).

In puppies the testicles tend to slide forward beside the penis and are often difficult to find. In Shetland Sheepdogs especially, the testicles are often difficult to locate when the dogs are puppies. I have often spent no little time, when judging a Sanction Match, in attempting to find the testicles of excited, and sometimes frightened, puppies that are but a few days more than three months of age.

I must caution stud dog owners to be careful of using drugs or injections to make the dog eager to mate or more fertile. They can have just the opposite result. The number of puppies born in any litter is not dependent upon the male's sperm, if the stud is healthy and fertile, but upon the number of eggs the bitch discharges. Should your male prove to be sterile, look for basic causes first. If there seems to be no physical reasons for his sterility, then a series of injections by your veterinarian might prove efficacious.

It is a good idea to feed the stud a light meal before he is to be used for breeding, particularly if he is a reluctant stud. Young or virgin studs often regurgitate due to excitement, if given food prior to the breeding, but this does no harm.

Remember that any stud dog can leave his mark genetically on the animals of the future in any given locale, and that long lasting impression can be either for good or ill. So use your stud dog well, do not breed him to questionable bitches, and always provide for a return service if the bitch fails to produce a litter from the breeding, or if she produces only a single puppy. Be as honest in your dealings with fanciers within your breed as your dog is honest in all he does.

It is a great pleasure, and can bring much satisfaction, to be the proud owner of a fine stud dog whose name will be remembered with reverence in the history of the breed.

When partners are selected for breeding it is
essential that they each balance and compensate
the hereditary faults and virtues of the other both
physically and mentally. To accomplish this end the
genetic formula of both dog and bitch must be
known to the breeder.

CHAPTER 8

SELECTION OF BREEDING PARTNERS

"Mens sana in corpore sano". A sound mind in a sound body; this is the aim of the true and honest breeder. To accomplish this design the selection of breeding partners is most important.

We must begin, of necessity, with the bitch, the mother, for she is the fountainhead for the breeder. She should be as fine a bitch as it its possible for you have bought or bred. You must make the effort to do some detective work and attempt to find out all you can about her sire and dam, their litter mates, and the litter mates of your bitch. Try also to find out what all these animals produced, and particularly what faults they produced. Faults are very important when considering breeding for, unlike judging when one looks for virtues, faults can be the ruin of our breeding hopes and must be known and assessed so that they can be eliminated.

Put all the data you have amassed about your bitch together, assort it and analyze it. Make a chart naming every part of the animal's body, and don't forget temperament, then, using symbols as a kind of shorthand, examine your bitch genetically and record your findings on the chart. Do not make the chart simple or you defeat your purpose, and remember, it can be used every time you breed this particular bitch. For instance under the overall heading of "Temperament", list: reaction to sharp sound, reaction to people (hand-shy or not), outgoing or not, playful or quiet (energy), reaction to strange environment, etc.

When your chart is completed you should know if your bitch carries recessives for a better croup, for example, than she displays, or if she can, from what you have gleaned of her genetic background, pass on to her puppies a longer and less desirable loin than she herself exhibits.

The chart you have made is just one of many you will have to make and, though the work is arduous you must gird your loins for further similar chores. The next chart you make will be of a mythical male dog who will compensate, or correct, the faults you know now are inherent in your bitch. This mythical dog is the perfect breeding partner for her.

Your final chart chore is to gather the names of all the stud dogs that you have been thinking of as mates for your bitch. Begin again with your charts and amass all the data that you can about each of the admired studs dogs and chart it, just as you did with your bitch. Now match the charts of the actual dogs with the chart of the mythical *ideal* stud dog . . . and you will be amazed at what you have learned, and the hidden faults carried by some of the best known studs. None of the living stud dogs will probably chart out as perfectly as the mythical dog, but the one that comes closest is the dog to pick for the next breeding to your bitch, unless there is some fault that you specifically wish to control in the bitch's breeding that the stud dog also carries.

You must come to grips with yourself and definitely decide what traits you consider absolutely essential and what faults intolerable, and use this yardstick against your charts to measure the worth of the stud you will select for the coming breeding. But never forget these essentials, which are necessary to all breeding success: *vigor, fertility, true breed character, and temperament.*

It is always best to breed to a tested stud dog, for much can be learned about the dog from the quality of his get. One cannot tell by *looking* at a dog the kind of youngsters he will sire and, because of this, the untried dog, no matter how fine he may be as an individual, is too much of a gamble as a stud.

Establishing a strain which bears the unmistakable touch of your own breeding genius, is the ambition of most breeders. Before we discuss how to do it, let us first define it. A strain is a family within a breed which possesses definite and individual characteristics which consistently breed true.

To breed animals to fit this definition, to develop a strain, the following recommendations, based mainly on the work of Humphrey and Warner, and Kelley and Whitney, can be used as a guide. The

Dog Name _____

Inbreeding _____

Date of Rating _____	broadly dominant	broadly recessive
Temperament _____		
To people _____		
To sound _____		
Environment _____		
Energy _____		
Misc. _____		
Teeth _____		
Bite _____		
Jaw _____		
Eye _____		
Ears _____		
Head _____		
Neck _____		
Prosternum _____		
Upper Arm _____		
Blade _____		
Angulation _____		
Pasterns _____		
Feet _____		
Rear Angulation _____		
Flare & Length Stifle _____		
HOCK _____		
Withers _____		
Back _____		
Loin _____		
Croup _____		
Tail Set _____		
Tail Length _____		
Size _____		
Weight _____		
Height _____		
Length _____		
Spring Ribs _____		
Length Ribs _____		
Depth Ribs _____		
Dry, Wet _____		
Bone _____		
Muscle _____		
Coat _____		
Pigmentation _____		
Hips _____		
Eating _____		
Sex Drive _____		
Movement _____		
Reach _____		
Drive _____		
Coming _____		
Going _____		

Comments:

This type of rating chart has been found useful by Fidelco Breeders, a group that breeds and supplies German Sheperd dogs to police and individuals requiring guard dogs. Information such as would appear on rating sheets of this type can be useful to breeders, regardless of what their breed is.

167

One cannot tell by just looking at this white Bull Terrier whether or not he will be a good sire. Unless a stud dog has been used enough so that his progeny can be assessed, breeding to him is a gamble.

first rule is exactly the same as the one proposed earlier in this chapter as essential in selecting the ideal breeding partners.

1. Decide what few traits are essential and what faults are intoler-able. Vigor, fertility, character, intelligence and temperament must be included in these fundamentals.

2. Develop a scoring system and score selected virtues and faults in accordance with your breeding aims. Particular stress should be put upon scoring for individual traits that need improving.

3. Line-breed consistently to the best individuals produced which, by the progeny test, show that they will further improve the strain. In-breeding can be indulged in if the animal used is of exceptional quality and exhibits no outstanding faults.

4. Relationship need not be close in the foundation animals, since wide outcrosses will give greater variation and therefore offer a much wider selection of desirable trait combinations. Later, outcrossing can be resorted to for the purpose of bringing in wanted characteristics that may be missing from the basic stock. Such outcrossing will destroy the homozygosity you have molded, so must be used with extreme care.

Every animal used in the program to establish a strain must, of course, be rigidly assessed for individual and breeding excellence and the excellence of its relatives and progeny.

The outcross breeding mentioned within the structure of the rules for founding a strain, should be used only when it is necessary to correct faults that the strain-line-breeding has made evident. When such outcrossing is utilized it should be considered a breeding thrown away, for the result will only be a tiny thread that you wish to weave into the tapestry of your strain. The outcross stud should

Sire and son may look very much alike, yet each will carry his own genetic formula and, though prepotency and linebreeding may enable both to pass on certain family traits, each is genetically unique.

be bred to the strain bitch who exhibits the closest breeding in your strain, and from the resulting progeny must be selected the animal that most closely resembles those of your pure strain, but shows improvement in the fault that was the reason for the outcross. From then on selection must be made to hold the improvement as you breed the animal from the outcross back into your strain line.

If at all possible it is best to develop two strains which, in type, complement each other, and both strains should have some genetic relationship. For instance, if your major strain is based on two or three crosses to a superb bitch which we will designate as "O", and two crosses to a very fine stud whom we will call "X", and these two animals were bred together to produce the exceptional "XO" who appears twice as a basic breed force in your strain, then the other strain you develop should employ either the "XO" animal or a litter mate as one of the breeding partners. The other partner should be an outcross that brings in corrective traits.

This second strain can feature those compensatory traits which you will establish through selection. Then, when the time comes when it is necessary to bring genetic repairs to your main strain-line, instead of finding it necessary to bring in a raw outcross with the resulting heterozygosity, you can blend in an individual from your second strain to achieve improvement without completely losing control over those characteristics which are the trade marks of your strain.

The owner of a popular stud dog can check out the litters his stud sires from a great variety of bitches and has the advantage of being able to assess the many breed types and how they produce to his stud. Using this data as a foundation he can build a strain with his stud as a base, utilizing as the other partner a bitch which he has found will give him the best stock from his stud. The bitch can either be leased for this purpose, or the stud dog owner can refuse a stud fee and select, instead, a fine puppy from the litter sired by his stud to be used as the F_2 animal in his proposed strain.

Do not be misled by hysterical misrepresentation in advertising when you are searching for a stud for your bitch. Do not view the dog labelled, "Champion" or "Imported", through a blind fog of ecstatic worship which completely hides the animal's faults and heritage. The implications of the myriad blind spots such selection can bring throw a long shadow of meaning. Remember that no

When selecting a breeding partner for your bitch, don't be misled by titles and tags such as, "Champion" and "Imported." By charting find the male best suited to your bitch genetically.

matter how great a dog may be he is not genetically right for all bitches, and you must not be led astray by glorified "tags" that indicate nothing of the dog's genetic heritage or what he can produce.

If you wish to breed for the market then the puppies sired by a well-known champion will sell more quickly and at better prices. But if you are earnestly going to attempt to better the breed and build a reputation for yourself, or a strain to bear your kennel name, you will breed for better purpose than the quick sale of expensive puppies.

The size of a kennel, the amount of money spent in stock or equipment, the number and quality of the dogs bought, shown, and won with, are no substitutes, in themselves, for the breeding skill that comes from knowledge and the patience to employ that knowledge to its fullest extent.

The male of the species should be strong and
noble, typical and filled with a zest for life and
the ability to do well the chore for which he was
bred. One look tells us that this Malamute stud is
fit and able to brave the icy winds of the white and
silent North.

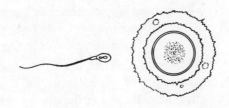

CHAPTER 9

THE MECHANICS OF BREEDING

The male dog and the bitch, like the opposite sexes of all animals, are ideally suited for the role they must play in the perpetuation of their species. We have learned how the bitch comes into season to make breeding possible, so now let us delve briefly into the mechanics of the act that is the supreme vehicle for genetic continuation.

When a bitch is brought to be bred to a stud dog the male "covers" the bitch; that is, he mounts her. He then indulges in a rhythmic pumping motion as he searches with his penis for the female's vagina. When the penis finds and is thrust into the vagina, it goes through a muscular ring at the opening and, as it passes into the vagina, pressure on the reflex nerves cause a violent thrust forward and the penis, and particularly the unique bulb which becomes enormously enlarged with blood, swells greatly preventing withdrawal through the restricting (constriction) band of the vulva. The stud begins to "tread", a frantic, surging, dancing movement of the feet similar to the movement of a swimmer who is treading water. He is, at that moment, ejaculating semen swarming with sperm, which is forced through the cervix and the uterus, into the fallopian tubes.

During copulation, the sperm are not just pumped out of the dog and into the bitch: they, the sperm (spermatozoa) are aided in their movement up the uterus by peristalsis, or waves of contraction passing along the uterus and forcing the contents (ejaculated sperm) onward. Within a very few minutes after sexual fusion (the tie) occurs, the sperm have travelled up the uterine passage, through the Fallopian tubes, and have found the capsule surrounding the ovaries. When sexual fusion occurs the semen is pumped from the male in spurts that probably coincide with the rhythm of his movement, and the bitch aids in keeping the male's penis enlarged through the regular tightening and relaxing of her vagina which is evidently caused by the series of peristaltic waves in the uterus.

Meanwhile, within the bitch, changes have been taking place that have led up to this moment. Eggs, developing in pockets that move toward the surface of the ovaries, have been ripened by germ plasm stored in the ovaries. On a specific day in the mating cycle of the bitch (generally from about the fourteenth to the eighteenth day), these follicles (the pockets) begin to protrude from the ovary (bean-shaped) and also produce follicular hormones which prepare the uterus for pregnancy. The walls of the follicles become progressively thinner which causes the follicles to protrude from the ovary and eventually, due to extreme internal pressure, they burst and liberate the ova (egg) into the capsule that surrounds it.

We will suppose that the breeding to the stud dog has already taken place, so that the sperm are swarming around the capsule. Like a conquering army, the sperm surround the ova, hundreds of thousands strong, armed with an enzyme which they hurl against the protective coating of the egg, wearing and weakening the outer layer until one tiny sperm finds an opening and, breaching the ramparts, rushes in to fertilize the egg.

Meanwhile, back at the kennel, the dog and bitch are tied, or "hung", and the active part of the breeding is completed. The owner of the bitch should stand at her head and hold her by the collar. The stud's owner should kneel next to the animals with his hand, or his arm or knee (if it is a large breed) under the bitch's abdomen directly in front of her hindquarters, to prevent her from suddenly sitting while still tied to the male. He should speak soothingly to the male and gently prevent him from attempting to leave his "mount" position on the bitch for a little while. Presently, when the stud begins to show evidence of restlessness, the dog can be helped off the bitch without breaking the tie. He can either be left standing next to her and still tied, or he can be gently turned by lifting one hind leg over the back of the bitch until the stud and bitch, still tied, are standing tail to tail. Some males are comfortable in this latter position and some in the former. Help him to achieve whatever position he seems to prefer.

Dogs remain in this "tied" position for various lengths of time after copulation, but ten minutes to half an hour is generally average.

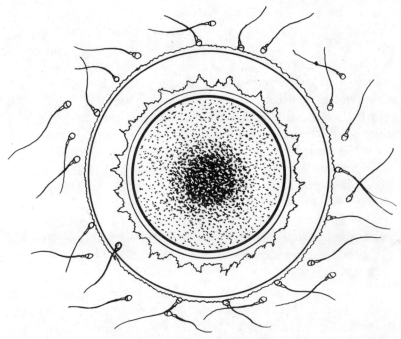

An egg, a special giant cell which the female ovaries produce, is here being assaulted by sperm which are attempting to pierce the envelope that surrounds the egg. The dark nucleus is the seat of the chromosomes, of which only half the required number are present. The first sperm to enter and reach the nucleus will bring with it the other necessary chromosomes for a normal cell number. Once inside the ovum the sperm will lose its tail. The nucleus of the egg is surrounded by growth enzymes.

When the congestion of blood leaves the penis, the bulb shrinks and the animals part. It is always desirable to have a "tie" when breeding. But sometimes the male cannot, or does not, force the swelling bulb section of the penis through the vaginal ring and is therefore not held. If this happens the stud owner should hold the male on the bitch and, by pressing the croup area of the dog, hold him so that his penis will not fall out of the vulva. If you can hold the dog in this position for approximately five minutes, the dog will discharge all of his sperm into the bitch with results similar to a five minute tie. While the stud owner holds the dog in position the owner of the bitch should hold her up so that she will not sink down and allow the male's organ to slip out. Breedings such as that which I have just described are almost always successful, that is if the bitch has been brought to the stud at the right time. Incidently, should the male fail to effect a tie and the penis and bulb are exposed while he ejects semen, it is best to allow him to mount the bitch and, once in the mount position, he will engage in the pumping motion which will aid in speeding the distention of the penis so that it will quickly subside and slip back into the sheath. The dog seems to be in no little discomfort when the penis is exposed in this manner and the moist, outer membrane begins to dry before the penis shrinks back into the sheath.

The stud dog owner should keep a muzzle handy to be used on snappy bitches. Many females, due to temperament, environment, or fright, may cause injury to the stud (or the humans involved in the operation) by biting. If a bitch shows any indication of such conduct she should be muzzled. Should she continue to snap and throw herself about, it could be because it is too early, or too late, in her estrus cycle to consummate a breeding.

If the bitch is small, sinks down when mounted, or won't stand, she must be held up. In some instances it will be necessary for the owner to slide his hand under her and, with his fingers, push her vulva up toward the dog's penis, or guide the stud's penis into her vulva. Straw, sand, or earth pushed under her hind legs to elevate her hindquarters, is effective in the case of a bitch who is too small for the stud. The hay or sand can be either loose or bagged.

The eggs, or ova, which the bitch has discharged move through the Fallopian tubes down into the uterus, whether they have been fertilized or not. If the breeding was successful and the eggs fertilized,

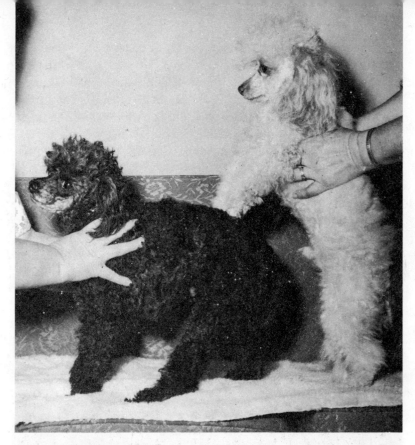

The breeding pair should be attended when about to copulate. This is particularly necessary if either of the pair is virgin. Dogs can be injured during the act of mating, or a young male ruined as a future stud if the bitch should vigorously resist him.

they become attached to the endometrium (uterine lining) and there, in their nest, proceed to grow. The eggs may even meet the sperm while on their downward journey to the uterus and become fertilized.

Within the bitch the corpora luteal hormone forms and brings the mating cycle to an end.

The male sperm and the eggs have united to form a new, living entity. The sperm supplying half of the forming whelp's genetic heritage, and the egg also offering half of the bitch's chromatic design. The chromosomes brought by sperm and egg pair off and the embryo becomes possessed of its own full complement of chromosomes packed with randomly selected genes.

I have previously mentioned artificial insemination as a means to an end if all other breeding attempts fail. The author has had good results with this type of breeding. One such breeding in which I used my imported stud dog, resulted in nine healthy puppies. Another time I artificially bred a bitch to a particular stud in Germany, had her shipped to me in Spain, where I had taken up residence, and the bitch whelped a fine litter of pups. I used this breeding practice several times with Beagles with good results, and I have heard many other breeders boast of their success in this area . . . and many, I must confess, whose results have been deplorable.

If you contemplate such a breeding, find a veterinarian who has had a good deal of practice at this sort of thing. He will probably use one or two tubes which are inserted into the vulva very gently and pushed slowly and deeply into the vagina. A small light will illuminate the vaginal canal so that the cervix (the end of the uterus) can be seen protruding from the top of the vagina. A syringe on which has been mounted a curved, long tube, smaller than the initial tube or tubes, is slid into and down the first tube used and the end of the curved tube inserted into the cervix. The syringe is the vessel which contains the semen, and the latter is released by a very gentle but

Infection is a common cause of sterility in dogs. Incidently the harlequin color pattern worn by this fine Great Dane is unique among canines and is a dominant modifier of black.

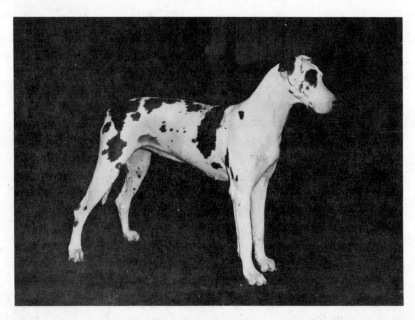

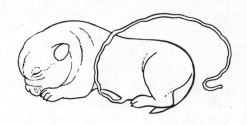

CHAPTER 10

THE RESULTS OF BREEDING

There is always a period of anxiety for the breeder after a bitch has been bred. Was the breeding a success? Is she pregnant? Will the results of this breeding be what we hopefully expect? During this interim period when none of these questions can yet be answered, the breeder can spend spare time rechecking charts and studying again all data and pedigrees, particularly the projected pedigree of the embryos the breeder hopes are now flowering in beauty within the bitch.

Occasionally fertile bitches, whether bred or not, will have phantom pregnancies and give evidence of every physical manifestation of true gestation up to the last moment. The abdomen enlarges, the mammary glands substantially increase in girth, and the bitch's appetite becomes typically greater. In some cases a bitch may be truly bred and then, about a month after the breeding, she may resorb her fetuses. This procedure is not at all uncommon in old bitches who often cannot any longer carry the developing embryos to full term. The difference between psuedo-pregnancy and fetal resorption can be determined by palpation, to locate the fetal lumps, if they are present, with your hands. But, as mentioned before, this is a difficult task to perform for one who has not had vast experience.

In the young and vigorous bitch who has been truly bred, the fertilized ova are developing in the horns of the uterus. The walls of the uterus keep pace in growth with the development of the forming embryos and the horns of the uterus lengthen in keeping with the number of eggs ripening within their confines. As the horns lengthen they contort and twist and snugly protect the rapidly enlarging embryos.

If you have read this far you know how cells divide until enough have formed to make the individual, and how the puppy receives his genetic recipe, his ancestral heirloom, through the two sets of chromosomes, one set from each parent, which arrived on the sex cells. During this early growth, and while the cells are still dividing to form the individual, one pair of cells segregate. These cells divide and increase independently of all the rest of the cells, for they are different from the other cells, they are the germ cells, the cells of future life, the genetic material that this forming individual will give to the next generation. These particular and special cells will become the most significant part of the gonads, the testicles or ovaries, depending upon the sex of the puppy, when it is born.

You, the breeder, begin to supply the environment for the puppies from the moment they are conceived. Whatever you feed the bitch is, in turn, processed and becomes food for the developing whelps. If you do not feed your bitch well and properly, nature will strip the bitch of her own nutrients to give to the pups and the bitch will become emaciated and rundown so that, even though the pups grow to full term and are whelped, the dam may not be able to sustain them due to the poor quality, or lack, of her milk.

I know that anyone who reads this book will give their pregnant bitch a proper diet, unless, of course, they are food faddists, and in that case I leave them to their own problems. It is, incidently, possible to predict with fair certainty, after the puppies are born, when your bitch ovulated and conception took place from this breeding. You can also determine if the puppies have arrived on time, prematurely or late, by checking the time their eyes open. The whelps will open their eyes ten days after the normal date of birth. This does not mean that they will be fully open, they will begin to open a tiny bit, just enough so that through the narrow slit the liquid glint of the covered eye can be seen. The eyes begin to open from the inside out and the lids will still be stuck together on the edges until the next, the eleventh day after birth.

Sometimes you will find that in one litter there are two groups of puppies, each opening their eyes at a different time, one group showing the virgin slit openings on the tenth day, the other on the eleventh day. You will also find that these two groups often vary

Whatever you feed your bitch during her pregnancy and afterward, while the young are being breast-fed, is reflected in the condition, health and vitality of the progeny in the nest. To fulfill their genetic heritage the whelps must be fed well before and after birth.

slightly in size. And sometimes there is even a greater period of time than just one day delay in the opening of the eyes between the two groups in the same litter. This phenomenon could be due to dual conception, and probably is. In the author's experience it has never happened in a litter born from a single breeding between the sire and the dam. Only in litters that are the result of multiple breedings, or more than one breeding, with a day skipped between services, have I seen this occur. Runts in litters could readily be the result of such multiple breedings, for once the bitch begins to whelp, the process of emptying all matter from her uterine tubes automatically continues until it is completed, and one or more puppies that were born from eggs fertilized by a second breeding, two days after the first, would be immature by that number of days, when born.

Now we have the puppies in the nest, healthy, grunting, squealing and suckling, all bellies and instinct and little more, except to the breeder, that is. To the breeder these lumps of living clay represent time, hope, and a big wish for the future. There is very little you, the breeder, can do in the first few weeks, except feed the mother well, check the puppies' navel against infection and, if you live in a cold climate, make sure that the pups are kept warm. This last is essential.

Dewclaws are the result of a simple recessive. In most breeds the dewclaws are removed, but Briards and Great Pyrenees, according to their accepted standards, must have double dewclaws on each hind leg.

A puppy that is chilled loses mobility, the strength to compete with litter mates at the dam's udders and, losing strength and resistance, succumbs.

If there is not adequate heat in the room where the whelping pen is located, heat should be supplied, during the cold months, through the agency of a room heater, small stove, an infra-red bulb rigged to hang just above the whelping box, or the new Goodyear pliotherm heating pads.

The puppies, which will become the progenitors of the future, may be born with dewclaws, the extra, or fifth, toe on the hind legs, a residual fixture from the past. In Great Pyrenees, and Briards, the breed standard calls for the presence of double dewclaws on the hind legs, and single ones on the front legs. In all other breeds the dewclaws on the hind legs should be removed by the breeder. This can be done by simply cutting the extra digits off with a pair of manicure scissors. A small pip of blood will rise to the surface which the bitch will lick off and within no time at all the site of the simple operation has healed. A good many breeds call for removal of the dewclaws on the forelegs also. These can be trimmed off in exactly the same manner as you employed in the removal of the rear dewclaws. Dewclaw surgery should be done the second day after birth. This is all generally, very simple, but there is one eventuality that must be reckoned with, and that is the tendency of some few bitches to lick the site of such a wound to such an extent that instead of healing it is kept bleeding.

Bleeding of this nature, or any kind of hemorrhagic action, no matter how slight, can bring tragedy to the young puppy. The dam's milk provides all the dietary factors necessary for the complete nutrition and explosive growth of her young. The puppy is *born* with a supply of iron, sodium and some other few minerals in an amount sufficient to last it until it is weaned, because these are the one group of nutritional essentials lacking in the dam's milk. If the very young whelp loses its precious store of iron and sodium through loss of blood, it will either become weak and unthrifty or it will die because these elements will not be replenished through the dam's milk.

During the weeks that must pass before the pups are old enough to cull and your own selection made to carry on your kennel name in the next generation, it is a good idea for the breeder to become

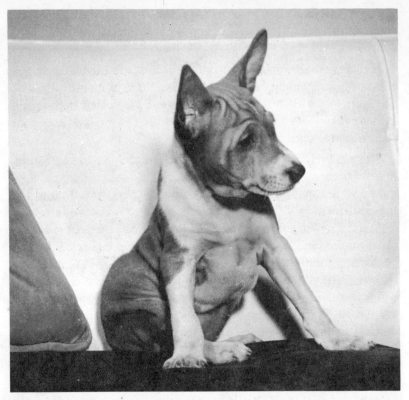

This Basenji puppy, like all canine youngsters, exhibits almost explosive growth in the limited time it has to reach the skeletal freeze that signals the end of bone development. Your veterinarian can protect the puppy with vaccines so that there is no lapse of growth through illness.

freshly conversant with some of the newest advances that have appeared in his hobby field. For instance, there is a new human measles vaccine for canine distemper that can be given to puppies at the age of three weeks or less. There are new and better specifics for worm eradication, some of them injections. Check with your veterinarian for the details on all the many new ways to protect your future breeding stock against the ills that canines are heir to.

When you begin to cull the litter so that you can select the pups you will sell and the one or two that you will keep, start at the bottom. Begin by separating the poorest of the lot and setting them aside. Compare those you have left, after dividing them into two groups, one of males, the other of females, against the standard. Then check

Culling is often difficult when the litter is of high quality, such as that exhibited by these Japanese Spaniels. Segregate the sexes first, then eliminate from the bottom. For future breeding stock select the animal that exhibits improvement where it is most needed.

them against the faults you have been trying to eliminate. If the best pup in the litter still retains the fault you have been attempting to purge from your stock then it is not of any use to you in your future program. Lastly, if the male puppy which you find the best is not equal to, or better than, his sire, or the best bitch puppy not an improvement over her dam, especially in that area that needs improvement in your stock, then they will not bring the necessary and hoped for virtues that you need for improvement. I realize that it is almost impossible to assess a young puppy to this degree. But the breeder who knows his own stock can tell whether or not wanted improvement has been achieved in the latest litter.

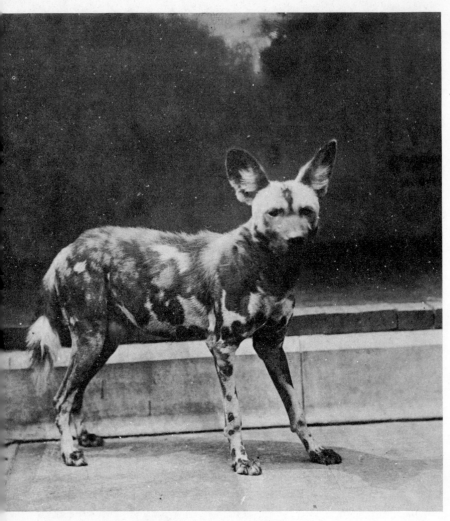

One of the most interesting of the wild dogs of the world is the Cape Hunting Dog of Africa, **Lycaon pictus.** Also called the South African Wild Dog and the Hyena Dog, it is unique in that it has only four toes on each foot and is the sole living species of its genus. Originally classified erroneously with hyenas, cats and civets, this wild dog with the strange, patchy coat, could be like a prehistoric, transitional canine.

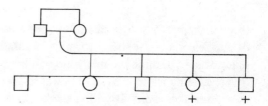

CHAPTER 11

ENVIRONMENT AND HEREDITY

There have been many theories advanced, as we have seen in earlier chapters, espousing the cause of environment as the prime factor in the evolution of species. Inevitably each such hypothesis has been proven false. An inexorable heredity that has been bequeathed to us from our ancestors through our parents, is the key to all we are and will ever be. Yet heredity is not an implacable destiny, holding forth decisions that cannot be appealed. For heredity determines the responses of the individual to the environment in which he exists and, in so doing, heredity can change not the individual, but in time, the race. It follows, therefore that, though environment cannot influence the individual's genetic material, or change that material, environment can select for certain specific genetic material within the confines of the race as a whole, and in the process of this selection, cause change in the hereditary factors of the race.

In this way all the many species of living things on earth today were developed. The key to the whole process lies in the vast and uncountable number of combinations that chromatic material can form, the genetic variety that is the basis of all races and life forms. From this vast vat of inheritable material that is a species, nature selects the individuals that best fit their environment to be the progenitors of the race. In this way environment and heredity work together to produce the most perfect creature for a specific time and place.

Since life first began upon the earth there have been trillions of billions of creatures, many of whom have left the imprint of their presence on this planet in the form of fossil remains. Nature has been lavish in the many forms she has allowed living creatures to don.

Then, like a child playing with toys, has grown tired of some and thrown them away. But basically there have been a specific number of species that have been forming through the millions of years, to eventually become the many races of living creatures that we know today. During those eons of molding to specific design, nature made many mistakes, animals within the confines of a particular race that departed from the norm of the species and died out because the pattern of their heredity could not fit into the design of the environmental stage on which they appeared to play their parts. The long extinct dinosaurs are an example of just such a species. During the long-ago Pliocene age, which ended a million years ago, more pertinent to this book, the canine-ursine mammals essayed gigantism by producing, Agriotherium, a monstrous bear that matured at over four feet at the shoulder, and an enormous dog, Amphicyon, king of the canine carnivores that hunted the plains of that ancient era. Amphicyon, as a race, died out because it was too huge for the species, and its genetic makeup was not pliable enough to invoke change to fit its environment.

Nature constantly selected within each species to forge an overall, natural economy. It was necessary that one species should prey upon another so that the rate of growth of any living group could be kept within bounds or there would be no room on the continents and in the seas for the enormous increase of living creatures. Or, as Darwin concluded, "A struggle for existence inevitably follows from the high rate at which all organic beings tend to increase".

Darwin did not mean a "survival of the fittest", in terms of tooth and claw battle. He meant in the ability to survive under adverse conditions, to breed and leave progeny to carry on the seed of the species. The mutual relations between living organisms and their environment is another science called, ecology, with which we are not concerned here. We are, at the moment not particularly interested in the fact that it required five thousand pounds of water to produce the grass that went into the making of the single pound of meat we fed our dog for dinner. We know that the chain of life is continuous, each living thing contributing to the continuity of other life forms. But all these facts make it clear to us how much heredity and environment are woven in the struggle for existence.

How can this help the breeder? He can learn from the past how to mold the genetic clay of the present and the future. Let us go

The sled dogs of the Arctic regions are true canine examples of Darwin's "survival of the fittest." Many breeds of dogs can be trained to be sled dogs, but only the true Northern breeds can survive the rigors of the Arctic terrain.

Selection for various coat qualities within the confines of specific breed type is illustrated by the rough and smooth coated collies. There is also a third Collie coat, a wiry hair type, sported by the Bearded Collie.

back for a few moments again, into the past when the earth was young, and examine a race of dogs that were the ancestors of the canine race of today. These predators, running in packs, were large, fierce beasts, rough but close-coated, for the plains on which they hunted were semi-tropical. Through gene mutation some of these early, wild canines carried a recessive for long, thick-haired coats, but due to the climate such coverings were detrimental to the few wild dogs in whom the recessive linked and produced the heavy coat. They became over-heated during the pack chase, fell behind and missed the kill and the subsequent feasting and full-bellied warmth and satisfaction of the end of a successful hunt.

Unquestionably the long-haired, feral dogs would become the victims of evolution's first law, "survival of the fittest". But the recessive persisted hidden deep in the genetic material of the race. Then, over a period of thousands of years, the winds sweeping the plains became sharper, colder. The tall, tender grasses of the plains were dispossessed by shorter, more wiry, hardier herbage, and the herbivorous creatures, hoofed and horned, that thrived on the grasses of the plains, began to change to accommodate, and get the most nutrients, from the new, tougher, green growth on the floor of the continents.

The huge ice sheets that sheathed Greenland, Siberia and northern Europe in crusts of excruciating cold began rapidly to thicken, grow and move, sliding away from their ancient moorings and marching inexorably to conquer and cover the world. On the plains the sharp, herald winds had fled away before the cutting cold of winter gales. Ice and snow came to the formerly semi-tropical clime that was the habitat of the dog packs. The animals of fleet foot that had been their former prey had changed with the coming of the snow and now must be cannily stalked through scent. The canines in their short coats shivered in the cold, blundered in their hunting, over-running the game and giving it the warning it needed to seek and find protection from the pack. Then the sleeping recessives came into their own. The long-haired dogs were not cold, their coats protected them, and their correlated slowness in the hunt was now an advantage. So nature selected to fit the environment and the close-coated, quick running canines died out, and the thick-coated, heavier, slower-running dogs carried the evolutionary banner of the species away from oblivion.

What you have read above in a few short minutes took nature thousands, perhaps hundreds of thousands of years to accomplish. Man has now taken over from nature, controlling the evolution of all the domesticated animals and plants. You, the breeder, shape the evolution of the breed you fancy, and you do it in the same manner in which nature performed her evolutionary miracles.

Let us relate to the premise we proposed occurred in primitive times, but move it to the modern era. We will suppose that a modern breeder of dogs becomes enamored of a short-coated breed. This breeder had formerly bred Collies and had always been keen on the beautiful, heavy, Collie coat. A New England dweller, the breeder finds that his newly acquired breed does not adjust well to winter's cold, white misdeeds, so prevalent during certain months in that particular area. His Collies had always wintered well, protected by their heavy coats. He wishes that his new breed possessed such coats, and he muses that as a matter of fact they would look well in heavier coats.

He has not delved too deeply into the geneology of this new breed and so is not aware that when the breed made its appearance, about a hundred years ago, long coated young sometimes appeared in litters, because during the formation of the breed a long haired breed, long established, had been brought into the stock to improve bone and temperament. Selection was made for the short-coated animals by the fathers of the breed, whose standard of perfection stressed a short and silky coat. Over the years, due to strict and ruthless selection and culling, fewer and fewer of the long-coated dogs made their appearance and, if they did, they were not mentioned by the breeders who, the minute they were born, eliminated them via the water bucket.

But, lurking in the germ plasm of some few individuals in the breed, were the recessives for long coats. Then, lo and behold, our breeder finds three youngsters with long coats in the whelping box. And these long-coated pups also possess wonderful bone and temperament. To make this Cinderella story short, our breeder selects for long coats and soon has a strain that have matched recessives for the trait and produce nothing but long coats. Being a highly gifted, wealthy and influential man with a beautiful daughter, our hero manages to have his longhairs recognized by the A.K.C. and the livid parent club of the breed (due to jealousy he subsequently leaves

Some Weimaraners carry a genetic recessive for the production of long, setter-like coats that is the result of the use of a setter-type hunting dog in the early stages of the breed's creation.

this club and forms a successful parent club of his own), and he and his long-hairs live happily ever after.

This successful gentleman did nothing more than nature had done a long time before him. He had selected for a type within the already formed breed structure that would better fit the environment to which he had brought it.

If you, the breeder, wish to bring any kind of change to your stock to better fit the breed standard, you must also do it by selection, but not necessarily to fit environment, for our domestic animals are no longer the genetic slaves to their environment since man can, and does, make the environment to fit the animal through his control of heat, air conditioning and the various food stuffs he feeds. Man then, now controls the reason for change in species; environment,

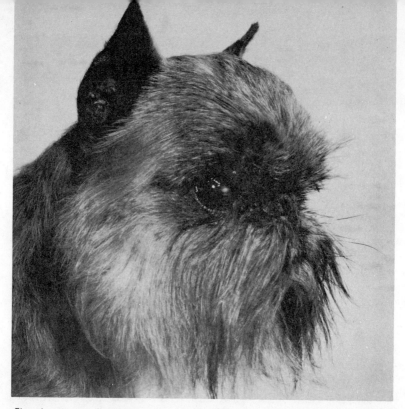

Though you may be breeding for smallness in Toys remember that diminutive size need not be synonomous with weakness. Select for vigor, fertility, vitality and the ability to survive.

and the means to change species; the knowledge of how to control heredity and manipulate genetic traits.

But, because man now controls the destiny of the canine race and not nature, it is necessary to constantly stress selection for those features which were the basics that nature insisted upon for the survival of the species; vigor, fertility, strength. Those animals that have any serious weakness die young in the wild, before they can reproduce and pass their weaknesses on. Those who have an advantage of some kind over their competitors or enemies, survive and breed and pass that advantage, genetically, on to their young. Natural selection weeds out the unfit, and preserves the fit. Man preserves the naturally unfit if they carry virtues that bring them closer to a man-made breed standard, and so basically he tends to weaken the breed. Yet even man will find it difficult to completely ruin a breed because of the variety that exists in genetic material.

Even litter mates, brought up in the same environment, respond in different ways to that environment, because of the difference in their genetic material.

If you are the breeder of a race of giant dogs, such as the Great Dane, and you have developed a strain that is very close to the breed standard and constantly produces this excellence, but is not consistently as tall at the shoulder as you want, how would you effect the necessary change to large size?

There are two avenues open to you. You can breed many more dogs, step up your breeding operations, so that you would have greater selection. Then you would have to constantly select for size in each litter. The trouble is that you would probably have to sacrifice some of the other excellencies that you have painstakingly stamped into your strain over the years when you select for size. Gradually over a period of many years, you will increase the size of your stock. But you might reach the end of your own existence before your stock

If you are breeding for great size use animals that exhibit this wanted virtue and whose forebearers were also known carriers of this characteristic.

No matter what the change you wish to bring into your line, longer ears, shorter legs like this Dachshund, greater size, etc., you will lose less in wanted type if the animal you choose for these improvements is related to your stock.

can be depended upon to consistently produce the size you want. Perhaps a mutation for size would occur and you could, in one fell swoop, reach your desired goal. But wishing for specific mutations do not make them appear, so looking for that one in a billion or more mutation, is whistling in the dark.

The other, and sensible, way to increase the size of your stock, is to breed to a stud of huge size, or buy or lease a bitch of great size, that is also good in type. Your job of repairing the damage this outcross will bring to the homozygosity of your line will be lessened if the animal you choose is related to your stock and mirrors the general type of your breeding. In this way the larger changes can be made in your strain, whether it's size, longer ears, shorter legs, or any other basic change.

But for the correction of small things, the job for the breeder is easier because of the pliability of genetic material. Watch for the small changes that materialize in the whelping box, the variance produced by the germ plasm. Be ready to recognize these small advances toward your ideal and use them to produce, in subsequent generations, the virtues you want.

When speaking of dogs, we no longer have to worry about environment verus heredity, for man himself makes the environment and plans the heredity. Look around you and you will see the amazing results of man's breeding acumen in other forms of livestock. Canaries, budgerigars, sheep, horses, cats, pigeons, cattle, etc. A multitude of strange, exotic, unusual varieties and breeds, developed by man from the basic wild stock by selection, and by taking advantage of every small mutation toward an envisioned ideal.

You, the breeder, have taken over from nature. The future of the breed, of the canine race, is in your hands. Those hands can raise, or they can destroy if they are not moved by knowledge. To you the future flings a challenge, and you must meet that challenge by keeping your breed strong and vital and not allowing insidious defects to become a part of its genetic picture. Nature would have found and eliminated those animals which, due to abnormal genes, will lower the fitness of the species to survive. Defective genes can pile up and make a mockery eventually of all our advances toward a breed ideal.

The pedigree of this Spaniel is a record of its forebears. Its importance lies in the knowledge the
reader or breeder may have of the type, utilitarian
ability, and breeding worth of the animals in the
pedigree.

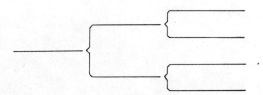

CHAPTER 12

THE IMPORTANCE OF PEDIGREE

A pedigree is a record of a dog's ancestry. It tells the owner the names of the sire and dam of his dog, the grandparents, the great-grandparents, and perhaps the great-great-grandparents. It is, in other words, a collection of names, a nebulous assemblage of letters that have no real meaning except as handy hooks on which to hang a boast.

There are pedigrees that do have value to the breeder, German pedigrees, issued for German Shepherd dogs in the country of their initial birth, that tell us how many litter mates this dog had, if any sported the taboo long coat, or were unsound through orchidism. We can learn how the parents and grandparents were rated by the breeding board, read a short and valuable description of these animals, with faults included, and the colors, ratings and names of their litter mates. We can glean some idea of their intelligence and trainability through the training degrees they have acquired. All this and other information can be had from a German pedigree. The pedigrees issued in this country tell us nothing but the names of the dog's ancestors.

Actually a pedigree can be made out for any dog, or any living thing, for to be alive they must have had parents and grandparents, etc., and the pedigree of even a crossbred mutt would be a record of its ancestry. What people mean when they ask about an animal's pedigree is proof of its *pure-bred* ancestry. In other words, are all this dog's ancestors of the same breed? Of course registration in the recognized stud book is approximate proof that the animal is pure-bred.

To the breeder a pedigree means a great deal more than this.

The ability of the gun dog to be steady on point, to have "bird sense" and the physical stamina to range wide and fast all day long, are all inherited characteristics that can be produced by the canny breeder.

Though it tells him nothing of the *genetic* values of the dogs named, it does impart an immediate assessment of the *quality* of the animals behind his dog. Surnames found in the pedigree are often clues of specific quality to breeders with long memories and an equally long time in the breed. Familiar names, the trademarks of well-known kennels, usually impart an immediate vision of a specific type which was the result of linebreeding or saturation within the kennel of the heritage of a particular stud dog.

The importance of a pedigree lies in the knowledge we have of the individual dogs involved. A fifteen or twenty generation pedigree may be an imposing looking document but it means nothing if we have no knowledge of the appearance or genetic qualities of the animals mentioned. It is of more importance to extend our knowledge of the first three generations than to extend the pedigree itself. These are the animals that count, the ones that appear in the first three generations. Beyond them the genetic picture would be too broad

Speed, heart and the competitive spirit, all necessary to the racing Greyhound, can be made negative by some slight physical anomaly such as a trifling lack of leg length, or too high a hock.

and too hazy to make its application to the dogs at hand pertinent. You will also find that what can be gleaned about the dogs of the past, and what they produced, has been distorted by time until there is very little of value or truth left. Photos of the animals, looking their best and then retouched beyond recognition, add nothing to the tiny sum total you may have found.

If you could piece together a picture pedigree for several generations, utilizing photos that have not been retouched, or with a minimum of retouching perhaps only through the background, it could prove to be of interest and value. Certain faults and virtues could be traced down, generation after generation, as seen and recognized in the photographs. Photos of litter brothers and sisters, when available, of the animals in the photos, would further enhance your knowledge, and you might possibly be able to tell what lines, within the sphere of your pedigree, have brought specific conformational excellence or faults mirrored in your own stock.

If you have hopes of reproducing the type of a particular and famous champion who appears several times in the linebred pedigree of your dog, it behooves you to carefully study his progeny in your pedigree. Were they typical of this dog? Did they mirror his type? Or were they atypical, with little of the famous dog's appearance? His beauty may have been the result of many recessives pairing and merging and becoming visible in the animal, then, through breedings with fine bitches of dominant heritage, this type could have become buried, no longer visible, with some of the recessives that had been responsible for his conformation, lost in his progeny.

Sometimes pedigrees are inadvertently, and without malicious intention, falsified. I know of several instances, in quite a few breeds, where plans had been made to breed a bitch to a specific stud. After the breeding had been made, the bitch had jumped the fence and been bred by another male, of the same breed, and in the same kennel. Often, in these cases, the second male was a son, or closely related to the preferred male used originally. The genetic pattern passed on to the progeny, therefore, could possibly seem to have been from the first male used since there was close relationship. Frequently the breeder had been absent when this last breeding took place, and the kennelman (or maid) did not mention it because it was due to his or her negligence that the incident occurred. Of course it was the last breeding that took, but the pedigrees of the puppies name the stud dog the bitch was initially bred to as the sire. When plotting a pedigree genetically, such an occurrence can certainly cause both difficulties and a warped picture of the inheritable material handed down to the animal you own.

If you have compiled rating charts such as I recommended in Chapter 8, you will have a very real and useful compilation of data that is immediately pertinent to your breeding problems. But it cannot be absolutely complete until you have collected like memoranda about the family behind your dog, the sire and dam and the grandparents.

Of real guidance in breeding is a card-index system, such as scientists use in plant and other animal genetic studies, and similar to that used in the Fortunate Fields experiment with German Shepherds, made by Humphrey and Warner. This system should indicate clearly the faults and virtues of every pedigree name for at least two generations, and three, if at all possible. It should also

The appearance of a dog, no matter how noble or "breedy," is no indication of his reproductive worth. Frequently there appears a line in his pedigree that causes anxiety to the very earnest and knowledgeable breeder.

record any back-massing in an earlier, the fourth or fifth, generation. Though the genetic influence of ancestors beyond the third generation is not of great consequence, and becomes an almost impossible-to-correlate maze due to the sheer number of names and the bulk of inheritable traits they represent, the massing of one dog's name in earlier generations can possibly alert us to watch for some inheritable defect (such as hip dysplasia).

The card-index system should also contain all available information about dominant and recessive traits (sectionally simplified) and the quality, in general, of each animal's progeny, with added notes in reference to the most prevalent virtues and faults of the progeny.

At the moment such a system would be difficult to achieve. There is little enough known about living animals, genetically, and the faults and virtues of dogs that are gone become distorted by time and sentiment. But, with a bit of digging, a little detective work, and a great deal of patience and questioning, of research and recording, some pertinent and valuable data can be brought to light about the names that compose your dog's pedigree. This is a real project and challenge that could, if engaged in, bring a vast fund of knowledge

The development of a card-index system for this Lhasa Apso would make its pedigree much more important, for it would record vital data about the animal's ancestors. Every breed could benefit from such data.

about a great many of the most important animals, not only in your dog's pedigree, but in the whole breed.

True pedigree recordings such as these, if correctly developed, can represent a really valuable contribution to breed knowledge and an invaluable recorded progeny test of ancestors. To be truly efficacious, near ancestors, as well as litter mates, must also be examined for endowed traits and percentages, in regard to these characters correlated and recorded in the pedigree index. From these indexes, graphs could be plotted which would indicate trends within the breed as a whole.

What a remarkable achievement it would be to have set up such a pedigree index accompanied by photographs of all the dogs named in the pedigree in the first few generations. No, it is not a dream, for I have seen it done and aided in its compilation. As one of the founders and officers of a foundation that is breeding dogs for specific utilitarian purposes, I have been one of a team that has compiled such data, very necessary in this case, for we are not commercial breeders and cannot afford to make mistakes or breed blindly. We can produce six to eight generation pedigrees, with full and concise

Prick-ear and drop-ear Skye Terriers are both recognized and eligible for showing, but would have to be bred specifically for the wanted ear if the characteristic is needed as a fixed genetic factor in the breed.

The future of your breed, whichever one of the many fine breeds it may be, rests in your hands, the hands of the breeder. The dogs to come will mirror your ability to utilize the tools science, experience, and breed knowledge have put into your hands to mold posterity for your particular breed.

data about most of the dogs named, and with illuminating photos of each dog. These descriptive, picture pedigrees, when spread out, will completely cover the floor of a large room. This could be called a breeder's dream—wall to wall pedigrees.

Always remember that in you, the breeder, is vested the power to fashion heredity, to mold life, in your chosen breed. You can use this power that creates life and change, that brings special life-forms into being, for good or ill. You must be aware of the power you have to design new patterns of heredity, and you must have the knowledge, the intelligence, and the integrity to use that authority well. If the future is to give us those things we each want for our respective breeds, we must clear our minds of inaccuracies and absorb truth instead, we must keep abreast of the advancing times and bring to our canine activities the newest scientific knowledge and achivements relating to the dog.

In the scheme of events that began so long ago, when the hirsute, arboreal ancestor of man swung down from the trees to begin his march of destiny to dominance over all the creatures of the world, it was written in those early stars that he would, someday, strip Mother Nature of her mantle of species evolution and drape it over his own shoulders.

You, the breeder, wear that section of Nature's cape of conjury that wove the intricate evolution of the canine species down through the ages of life. I have endeavored, in this book, to help you to wear it well, and with pleasure and dignity. If I have achieved my purpose, even in some small way, I rest content.

Finis coronat opus

GLOSSARY OF GENETIC TERMS AND SYMBOLS

It is difficult to entirely eliminate the scientific terminology which is an integral part of the study of genetics. Certain terms and symbols have specific definition and are consistently used for clarity. The following definitions will aid the lay reader to better understand these terms and symbols. They appear in alphabetical order.

ALLELE *(noun)*. A gene, factor, trait, which differs from its sister gene. *(See* allelomorphs).

ALLELOMORPHS *(noun; adj.* allelomorphic). Genes, factors, traits or types which segregate as alternatives. Contrasting gene pattern.

AUTOSOMES *(noun; adj.* autosomal). Paired, ordinary chromosomes, similar in both sexes, as differentiated from the sex chromosomes.

CHROMOSOMES *(noun)*. Small, microscopic bodies within the cells of all living things which serve as packets for the genes. When division of cells begins the chromosomes appear as short strings of beads or rods.

CROSSING-OVER *(noun)*. An exchange of factors of inheritance or genes between related chromosomes.

DOMINANT *(adj.)*. A trait or character (genetic) that conceals its twin recessive character. Generally visible. Indicates that a trait contributed by one parent conceals that from the other parent. Example: dark eyes are dominant over light eyes.

EPISTASIS *(noun; adj.* epistatic). Similar to hypostasis and like dominance, but epistasis occurs between factors not alternative or allelomorphic.

FACTOR *(noun)*. A simple Mendelian trait or character: may be considered synonymous with gene.

F_1 Represents the first filial generation. The progeny or "get" produced from any specific mating.

F_2 The symbol used to denote the second filial generation, or the progeny or puppies produced from a breeding between a male and female of an F_1 breeding.

GAMETE *(noun; adj.* gametic). A sperm or egg with half (haploid) its number of chromosomes. Also: a matured germ cell.

GENE *(noun; adj.* genotypic). A single unit (or determiner) of inheritance.

GENOTYPE *(noun; adj.* genotypic). The hereditary composition of an individual life form (dog). The sum total of every dog's dominant and recessive traits.

GET Puppies or offspring. Progeny.

HETEROZYGOUS *(adj.)*. Possessing contrasting genes (or allelomorphs). Where dominant and recessive genes are both present and paired.

HOMOZYGOUS *(adj.)*. Pure for a given trait or possessing matched genes for that trait. The opposite of heterozygous. (Thus inbred strains are said to be homozygous and outcross bred dogs are considered heterozygous. Degree must be substantiated.)

HYPOSTASIS *(noun; adj.* hypostatic). The masking of the affect of another factor, not an allelomorph. Example: masking of the ticking factor in dogs by a solid color that covers the areas that would appear ticked.

MEIOSIS *(noun)*. Cell division when egg cells or sperm cells are formed. The chromosomes do not split before division so that the egg or sperm cell formed has only half the original number of chromosomes.

MITOSIS *(noun)*. The process of normal cell division in which the chromosomes split so that each cell has the same compliment of chromatic material as the original cell.

PHENOTYPE *(noun; adj.* phenotypic). The external appearance of an individual. The outward manifestation of all dominant genetic material (or double recessive material. *See* recessive).

RECESSIVE *(adj.)*. A trait or character that is concealed or hidden by a like or matching dominant character. Exception: when no dominant is present and recessive genes pair for a given trait. Example: the fawn color of many breeds such as, Great Danes, Boxers, etc. which is the result of a double recessive. Paired recessives equal visibility.

ZYGOTE *(noun)*. The full complement (diploid) number of chromosomes in the fertilized egg. Also: a cell formed by the union of two sex cells.

♂ Indicates a male. The symbol represents the shield and spear of Mars, the God of war.

♀ Indicates a female. This symbol represents the mirror of Venus, the Goddess of love.

× Means "with", "between", etc. Symbol of a mating between any male or female.

BIBLIOGRAPHY

Arenas, N., and Sammartino, R., *Le Cycle Sexuel de la Chienne*. Etude Histol. Bull. Histol., 1939.

Ash, E. C., *Dogs: Their History and Development*, 2 vols., London, 1927.

Auerbach, Charlotte, *The Science of Genetics*, Harper and Bros., 1961.

Barrows, W. M., *Science of Animal Life*, N.Y., World Book Co., 1927.

Bateson, W., *Mendel's Principles of Heredity*, Cambridge Univ. Press, London, 1909.

Burns, Marca, *The Genetics of the Dog*, Comm. Agri. Bur., England, 1952.

Darwin, Charles, *The Origin of Species* and *The Descent of Man*, Modern Library, 1936.

——— and Wallace, A. R., *Evolution By Natural Selection*, Cambridge Univ. Press, London, 1958.

De Vries, Hugo, *The Mutation Theory* (vols. I & II), Open Court Pub. Co., 1909.

Dunn, L. C. and Dobzhansky, T., *Heredity, Race and Society*, N.Y., 1946.

Evans, H. M. and Cole, H. H., *An Introduction to the Study of the Oestrus Cycle of the dog*. Mem. Univ. Cal., Vol. 9, No. 2.

Fisher, Sir Ronald Aylmer, *The Genetical Theory of Natural Selection*, Clarendon Press, Oxford, 1930.

Hart, E. H., "Artificial Insemination." *Your Dog* (March, 1948).

——— "The Judging Situation." *Your Dog* (March, 1948).

——— 1950. Doggy Hints. Men Mg. Zenith Pub. Co.

——— "Judgment Day." *Shep. Dog Rev.* (Jan., 1953).

——— *This Is The Puppy*. T.F.H. Publications, Inc., New Jersey, 1962.

——— *Encyclopedia of Dog Breeds*. T.F.H. Publications, Inc., 1966.

——— *How To Train Your Dog*. T.F.H. Publications, Inc., New Jersey, 1966.

——— *Dog Breeders Handbook*. T.F.H. Publications, Inc., New Jersey, 1966.

——— *Your Shepherd Puppy*. T.F.H. Publications, Inc., New Jersey, 1966.

——— *This Is The Weimaraner*. T.F.H. Publications, Inc., New Jersey, 1965.

——— and Goldbecker, W., *This Is The German Shepherd*, T.F.H. Pub. Co., Inc., N.J., 1955.

Hermansson, K. A., *Artificial Impregnation of the Dog*, Svensk. Vet. Tidshr., 1934.

Humphrey, E. S. and Warner, Lucien, *Working Dogs*, Baltimore, Johns Hopkins Press, 1934.

Hutchins, C. M., *Life's Key—DNA*. Coward-McCann, 1961.

Krushinsky, L. A., *A Study of the Phenogentics of Behavior Characters in Dogs*, Biol. Jour. Zool. Moscow State Univ., 1938.

MacDowell, E. C., *Heredity of Behavior in Dogs*, Dept. of Genetics, Yearbook,

Morgan, T. H., *Evolution and Adaptation*, Macmillan, N.Y. and London, 1903.

——— *The Mechanism of Mendelian Heredity*, Henry Holt, 1933.

Pearson, K. and Usher, C. H., *Albinism in Dogs*, Biometrica, 1929.

Razran, H. S. and Warden, C. J., *The Sensory Capacities of Dogs*, (Russian Schools), 1929.

Robson and Henderson, *The Action of Estrus on the Bitch*, London, 1936.

Simpson, G. G., *Life Of The Past*, Yale Univ. Press, 1961.

Stockard, Chas. R., *The Genetics of Body Form and Type in Breed Crosses Among Dogs*, Proc. 6th Internat. Cong. Genetics, 1932.

Tehver, J., *When Is The Heat Period Of The Dog?* 1934.

Whitney, Leon F., *The Basis Of Breeding*, Fowler, 1928.

INDEX

INDEX

A

A.K.C., 162
A.P.L., 162
Abdominal Rings, 160
Aborting, 148
Acceptance Period, 141
Acid Milk, 153
Acquired Characteristics, 23
Advertising, 170
Afterbirth, 149
Agriotherium, 190
Alleles, 45
Amino Acids, 68, 69
Amniotic Fluid, 149
Amphicyon, 190
Anorchidism, 160
Anthropoids, 22
Antibiotics, 179
Appetite, 147
Aristotle, 22
Artificial Insemination, 162, 177, 179
Asters, 49

B

Back-massing, 133, 206
Backcrossing, 125
Bacteria, 150
Basset Hound, 32
Beagles, 178
Bedding, 147

Birthmarking, 37
Bleeding, 185
Blood, 40
Breast, 151
Breeding Depth, 96
Breeding Terms, 40
Briards, 185
Brood Bitch, 137
Brunn Society For the Study Of
    Natural Science, 31
Budgerigars, 134
Bulldog, 14

C

Calcium, 144, 152
Calcium Gluconate, 153
Camphorated Oil, 153
Canis familiaris inostranzewi, 14
Canis familiaris intermedius, 14
Canis familiaris leineri, 14
Canis familiaris metris-optimae,
    14
Card-Index System, 204, 206
Castration, 162
Cenozoic Era, 12
Centrioles, 49
Cereal, 144
Cervix, 173, 178
Character, 166
Charts, 165
"Checks," 93
Chihuahua, 14

Chromatic Gene Packet, 64
Chromosomes, 40, 44, 45, 49, 52,
    53, 64, 76, 177
Chromosome Pairs, 64
Coat Color, 32
Collies, 194
Columbia University, 40
Concentrated Inbreeding, 120
Copulation, 140-143, 158, 160,
    173, 174
Cord, 151
Corpora Luteal Hormone, 177
Correction, 84
Corrective Breeding, 132
Corrective Traits, 170
Crossing-Over, 61, 64
Cryptorchidism, 52, 160, 161, 162
Cynodictis, 13
Cycle, 140, 141
Czardas V. Eppeleinsprung-Noris,
    156

D

DNA, 68, 69
Darwin, Charles Robert, 22-25,
    28, 33, 69, 190
The Descent of Man, 22
Deoxyribonucleic Acid, 68
Determiners, 28, 29
De Vries, 33, 40
Dewclaws, 185
Difficult Whelpers, 150
Discharge, 140
Distemper, 18

Dominant, 28, 45, 64, 85
Dominant Allele, 45
Dominant Color, 29
Drosophila melanogaster, 40, 61
Drugs, 104, 162
Dual Conception, 183

E

Eclampsia, 152
Ecology, 190
Egg, 49, 160, 163, 174, 177
Egyptian House Dog, 14
Embryos, 182
Emission, 160
Endometrium, 177
Environment, 22, 64, 73, 189,
    190, 193, 195, 197
Eocene Period, 12
Epididymis, 159, 160
Epistasy, 64
Epistatic Factor, 64
Establishing a Strain, 166, 169
Estrus Cycle, 176
Evolution, 194
Exercise In The Prenatal Period,
    146
Experiments In Plant
    Hybridization, 31
Eye Color, 81
Eyes, Opening of, 182, 183

F

Fallopian Tubes, 146, 173, 176

Fat, 144
Feeding, 139
Fertility, 108, 166, 196
Fertility Drugs, 142
Fetal Development, 144
Fetal Envelope, 149
Fetal Lumps, 181
Fetal Resorption, 181
Fisher, Sir Ronald Aylmer, 40
Flowers, 27
Focke, W.O., 33
Follicles, 140, 174
Formula For The Biological
    Laws, 29
Fruit Flies, 40, 44, 57, 61

G

Galton, 25, 32
Gamete, 52
Garden Pea, 28
Genes, 37, 40, 44, 45, 53
Genetics, 33, 44
Genetic Background, 165
Genetic Composition, 64
Genetic Deafness, 96
Genetic Experiments, 120
Genetic Mutations, 61, 193
Genetic Ratios, 89
Genotype, 73, 85
Genotypic Characters, 73
Germ Plasm, 57, 89, 121, 174,
    198
Germ Cells, 182
German Shepherd Dog, 57, 201
Gestation, 146, 152

Giant Dogs, 197
Glands, 148, 152
Gonads, 182
Great Dane, 57, 197
Great Pyrenees, 185
Greyhound, 14, 23
Grimm von der Fahrmuhle, 108,
    156

H

Haldane, 40
Heat, 137, 139, 185
Hemophilia, 53
Hereditary Units, 29
Heredity, 23
Heterosis, 120, 133, 135
Heterozygosity, 130, 170
Heterozygous, 45, 53, 131
Heterozygous Young, 116
Hip Dysplasia, 96, 206
Homozygosity, 116
Homozygous, 45, 53, 80, 96, 133
Hybrid, 28, 29
Hybrid Vigor, 120
Hybridization, 27
Humphrey, 166, 204
Huxley, Sir Julian, 44

I

Implements Used During
    Whelping, 150
Inbreeding, 116, 117, 121, 124
Infection, 179

Inheritance of Acquired
    Characters, 37
Injections, 163
Irish Wolfhound, 14
Iron, 144, 185

K

Kelley, 166
King, Dr. Helen L., 117
Knight, 32

L

Labor, 149
Lamarck, Jean-Baptiste, 22, 23,
    37
Laws of Heredity, 31
Lebistes reticulatis, 117
Lethal Faults, 121
Lethal Factors, 134
Lethal Genes, 96
Line-Breeding, 125, 129, 130, 202
Liver, 146
Longevity, 108
Luteal Bodies, 148
Lysenko, 22, 37

M

Maiden, 142
Maiden Bitches, 141
Male Lines of Descent, 155

Male Organs, 159
Mammalian Carnivores, 12
Manipulation, 179
Mastiff-type Breeds, 14
Mastitis, 153
Mating Cycles, 138, 143, 144, 177
Meat, 144
Mechanics of Breeding, 173
Meiosis, 52
Mesonyx, 12
Mesozoic Era, 11
Metabolis Disturbance, 152
Mendel, Gregor Johann, 26, 27,
    32, 33, 37, 69
Mendelian Expectation Chart, 28
Mendel's Units, 45
Miacis, 13
Mice, 27
Michurin, 37
Michurinian Theory, 37
Milk, 144, 151, 152
Minerals, 144, 185
Miocene Era, 14
Mitosis, 45, 49
Mixed Paternity, 144
Monorchidism, 52, 160, 161
Morgan, Thomas Hunt, 44
Muller, H.J., 44
Mutational Effects, 133
Mutations, 33, 44, 57, 60, 64, 81,
    135, 198
Muzzle, 176

N

Natural Evolution, 80

Natural Selection, 25, 196
Nausea, 151
Navel, 183
Navel Cord, 149
Nerves, 160
Neurosporacrassa, 57
Norm, 105, 108, 109, 157
Nucleic Acid, 64
Nucleotides, 69

O

Oligocene Period, 12
Opposing Allele, 52
The Origin Of Species, 22
Orchidism, 52, 161
Ova, 140
Ovarian Follicles, 141, 148
Ovarian Hormones, 148
Ovaries, 140, 173, 174
Ovulation, 141, 142
Ovum, 52
Outcross Breeding, 112, 116, 130-132, 169, 198

P

Paleocene Age, 12
Palpation, 146, 181
Pangene, 24
Pangene Theory, 25
Pangenesis, 32
Partial Dominance, 64
Pedigree, 129, 130, 201-207
Pelvis, 149

Penis, 141, 143, 144, 160, 173, 174, 176
Peristalsis, 173
Peristaltic Waves, 174
Peritoneum, 162
Persian Herd Dogs, 14
Pfeffer v. Bern, 156
Phantom Pregnancies, 181
Phenotype, 73, 85
Phosphorus, 144
Pitocin, 151
Pituitary, 148
Pituitrin, 151
Placenta, 139, 148-150
Pliocene Age, 190
Pregnancy, 146, 147
Prepotency, 116, 129, 132
Primrose Plants, 33
Progesterone, 148
Prolactin, 148
Prostate Gland, 160
Proteins, 68, 69
Provisional Hypothesis of Pangenesis, 24
Ch. Pulaski's Masterpiece, 156
Pure Dominant, 28
Pure Recessive, 28

R

RNA, 68, 69
Radiation, 44
Railing, 147
Rating Charts, 204
Reasoning, 100, 101
Red Brucie, 155, 156

Relaxin, 148
Reproductive System, 142
Resorbtion of Fetuses, 153
Return Service, 163
Recessive, 28, 45, 89, 162, 194,
      204
Recessive Allele, 45
Recessive Characteristic, 52
Recessive Traits, 85
Ribonucleic Acid, 68
Runts, 183

Standards, 80
Sterility, 61, 160, 163, 179
Stilbestrol, 153
Strength, 196
Strain, 166, 170
Strain-Line-Breeding, 169
Stud Dogs, 155, 157
Stud Fees, 156, 170
Sutton, W.S., 40

T

Telegony, 37
Temperament, 109, 137, 166
Temperature, Drop in, 149
Test Breeding, 96
Testicles, 52, 159, 160, 162
Thales, 22
Tie, 141-144, 173, 174, 176
Tomarctus, 13, 14, 16
Toy Breeds, 138
Trait, 28
Type, 155

S

St. Bernard, 14, 76
Sac, 149, 151
Saturation, 37
Scoring System, 168
scrotum, 52, 160, 162
Selection, 23, 117
Semen, 160, 173, 176, 179, 179
Seminal Vesicle, 159
Selection Of Breeding Partners,
      165
Sex Cells, 24, 28, 49
Sex-Linked Diseases, 53
Sex-Linked Traits, 52
Sexual Fusion, 173
Sight Hounds, 14
Sodium, 185
Somatic Cells, 49
Sperm, 49, 141, 159, 160, 162,
      163, 173, 176, 177, 179
Sperm Count, 179
Spermatozoa, 52, 160
Spermatozoon, 49

U

Umbilical Cord, 149, 150
Uneven Dominance, 93
Uniformity, 131
Units, 28, 40
Units Of Heredity, 44
University of Amsterdam, 32
Upgrading, 108
Uterine Passage, 173
Uterus, 146, 173, 174, 176, 181

V

Vaccine, 186
Vagina, 173, 174, 178
Vaginal Canal, 178
Vaginal Ring, 176
Vaginal Smear, 142
Vas Deferens, 160
Vas Deferentia, 159
Vigor, 108, 196
Virgin Bitches, 143
Virgin Studs, 163
Vitamins, 144, 179
Vitamin and Mineral
 Supplements, 144
Vulva, 140, 141, 143, 176, 178

W

Warner, 166, 204

Weaning, 153
Weismann, 25
Whelping, 149-152
Whelping Box, 147, 185
Whitney, Dr. Leon F., 117, 166
Wire Fox Terrier, 64
Worm Eradication, 186
Wright, Sewell, 40

X

XX, 45
XY, 52
X Chromosome, 45, 52, 53
X-Rays, 44, 57, 146

Y

Y Chromosome, 45, 52

INDEX OF COLOR ILLUSTRATIONS

Affenpinscher, 82
Afghan Hound, 62
Australian Terrier, 75
Basenji, 102
Bedlington Terrier, 74
Belgian Sheepdog, 95
Bichon Frise, 111
Black and Tan Coonhound, 94
Borzoi, 42
Boston Terrier, 107
Bouvier des Flandres, 98
Boxer, 119
Brittany Spaniel, 66
Bulldog, 103
Bullmastiff, 123
Bull Terrier, 43
Cardigan Welsh Corgi, 118
Cavalier King Charles Spaniel, 126
Chinese Crested, 39
Chow Chow, 90
Clumber Spaniel, 127
Dachshund, 122
Dalmatian, 38
Doberman Pinscher, 51
English Cocker Spaniel, 79
Flat-coated Retriever, 59

Fox Terrier, 47
Golden Retriever, 34
Gordon Setter, 46
Great Dane, 59
Great Pyrenees, 50
Irish Setter, 91
Irish Wolfhound, 67
Italian Greyhound, 106
Keeshond, 99
Kerry Blue Terrier, 127
Komondor, 35
Labrador Retriever, 55
Lhasa Apso, 47
Papillon, 54
Pomeranian, 43
Poodle, 63
Pug, 87
Rhodesian Ridgeback, 70
Rottweiler, 115
Saint Bernard, 114
Saluki, 71
Samoyed, 83
Schnauzer, 110
Shih Tzu, 78
Viszla, 58
Whippet, 86

OUR DOG BOOKS HAVE THE ANSWERS!

When you have a question that concerns your dog's health or well-being or your own enjoyment of him as a well-trained, responsive companion, you need authoritative, practical answers . . . and you need them fast.

T.F.H. Publications, Inc., the world's largest and most respected publisher of good literature about pets, publishes good books that answer just about all of the problems that confront dog owners. Whether your questions are about individual breeds or specific areas of dog-related interest, such as showing dogs, health care, or breeding dogs for profit, T.F.H. publishes a book that will enable you to make your dog healthier, happier, better-behaved and better-appreciated—and to make dog ownership easier, more pleasurable and more economical for you.

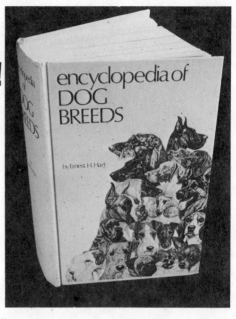

ENCYCLOPEDIA OF DOG BREEDS, by Ernest H. Hart. This is the most complete all-breed dog book ever written. Every recognized breed as well as many that are virtually unknown in America is illustrated and discussed. The book contains six large color sections and a wealth of black and white photos and line drawings. History, management and care of all dogs is included along with new and fascinating breed information.

visit your pet shop today or write for a complete book list of all T.F.H. books about dogs and other pets.
T.F.H. PUBLICATIONS, INC.
P.O. Box 27
Neptune City, NJ 07753